BELIEVE & ACHIEVE

Kulin Desai

BELIEVE & ACHIEVE

BELIEVE & ACHIEVE
© Kulin Desai 2018

First Edition 2016

CR94927
For existing IBOs only. Not for use with prospects.

Dedication

This book is dedicated to my mother. Without her, I would not have been able to become the person that I am today. She was an embodiment of strength, confidence, determination, and courage. She is my real hero. Observing her confidently and positively sail through the tough times only increased my admiration and love for her. I know she is showering her blessings from heaven on my family and me. Mom, I love you and miss you.

CONTENTS

FOREWORD

In life, most people equate success and happiness with wealth. What they fail to realize is that success and happiness come from a combination of five aspects: wealth, good health, great relationships, a profession or career that you love, and a strong spiritual foundation.

Believe & Achieve is not just another self-help book based on theory. It gives you a very common-sense and practical approach to betterment on the journey to success. It breaks down complex ideas into their simplest form, making it easy for anyone to understand. The real-life examples and straightforward style of the book make it a thought-provoking and enjoyable read. I strongly encourage everyone to read and apply the principles in this book to fulfill your goals.

When we first met Kulin, over 25 years ago, we knew him as a professional who was just starting his transition into an entrepreneur. We've seen him apply the success principles he outlines in his book to not only become an accomplished entrepreneur, but also to take giant strides forward in his health, relationships, career, and spirituality.

— Kanti Gala

ACKNOWLEDGMENTS

This book is a direct result of the love and encouragement that I have gotten over the years from my family and friends.

To my older siblings, Jyotiben, Asha, and Vikas. Thank you for supporting and guiding me through all of life's situations. I wouldn't be where I am today without you three. Mom would be proud of us.

To Vithhalbhai, the elder brother my siblings and I needed during our difficult time. Thank you for being there for our family when we needed it the most and for helping us get back on our feet.

To my wonderful wife, Mina, who has been a rock-solid support to me during the days of trial and triumph. Your love and support has made me who I am today. I am blessed to share with you this wonderful journey together filled with lots of joy and happiness. We've built a beautiful family together: our wonderful son Kavan, lovely daughter-in-law Anjali, precious daughter Mona, and joys of our life, our grandchildren Nikhil and Sia.

To my son, Kavan, who is the most considerate person that I have ever known. Over the years, you have grown to be a fine young man who makes me proud every moment. Thanks for bringing beautiful Anjali into our life; she has been our second daughter. You have helped me in more ways than I can list here. I thank you and encourage you to never lose the vision that you have created for you and our family. You are truly a winner!

To my daughter, Mona, who is the most precious person in our lives. We have created so many fond memories over the years that will last forever in my heart. You are the most loving and understanding person that I have known. I want to thank you for the countless hours that you have spent helping me write this book. Your mom and I are very proud of you. You are indeed the most wonderful daughter a parent could have. A lucky young man will someday take you away from me, but you will always be my little 'Monu.'

To my grandchildren Nikhil and Sia, the sun rises and sets for me in your faces every day. Your laughter and all the silly things you make me do fill my life with joy. Our home feels so lonely when you both are not around. Nothing has brought more happiness to me than the two of you. You have taught me the true meaning of unconditional love. You two are the love of my life.

To my best friend and mentor, Kanti. You have been the father figure to me that I never had. Thanks for guiding me in life and teaching valuable lessons that have helped me become the successful person that I am today. I can never fully repay you for the kindness, support, and guidance that you have provided to Mina and me. Thanks to Kanti and Lata for the encouragement and for being our friends in spite of our shortcomings.

PREFACE

My intent in writing this book is to share with you the universal laws of success that I have learned to apply in my life. Having witnessed for many years the struggle many individuals face in their journey to success, this book is for those who have seemingly fallen in a rut and are perhaps unsure of what got them there. My goal is to help such individuals unlock the doors of happiness and success and to allow them to see how the very laws of the universe can transform their lives.

This book is also for people who believe that others are more successful than they are simply because they were lucky and were in the right place at the right time. But there is no such thing. It does not happen by chance and it is no coincidence.

It has been said in so many ways by many great men and women over the last five thousand years of recorded history that we are what we think about. What we think about depends on our beliefs, expectations, and imagination. Circumstances are then attracted to you based on the above.

You may be thinking, "Oh! Not another book on the natural laws of success," and if you are, I don't blame you. I have read countless books on the subject myself and have felt that something was lacking. That was when I decided to write a book that provides practical examples of how to apply the laws with testimonies of how it has worked for me and for others. My goal is to not only help you understand these laws but also to teach you how to apply them in your own day-to-day life.

When you buy a computer, it comes with a user's manual. Unfortunately, the best computer in the world, your mind, does not come with one. You have to learn to use it well on your own. My sincere hope is that this book becomes the manual you are looking for and that it helps you make the most of your mind.

This manual is based on the four laws of success:

   1. The Law of Belief

   2. The Law of Expectation

   3. The Law of Imagination

   4. The Law of Attraction

The people who succeed at their goals and dreams understand, either consciously or unconsciously, these four universal laws of success, which work whether we are aware of or believe in them or not. They work no matter how hard we try to disprove them. Like the laws of gravity and magnetic attraction, the laws of success are universal and are always at work. It is in our best interest to make them work for us. That is what the Wright brothers did when they invented the airplane. They were able to fly because they worked with the law of gravity, not against it.

With the correct understanding and practice of these laws, one can easily acquire the success and happiness that they desire. These laws are simple and, when applied correctly, can shape your destiny, and you can experience a blossoming of abundance in all areas of your life. It's important to know that there is no limit to how blessed and happy you can be. Just believe.

Success or failure in life is based on our belief system. Let me explain. Belief is a trigger that starts a series of events to prove that what you believe is right. For example, in some cultures, people believe that when they see a black cat cross their path, something bad will happen. Based on this belief they will start expecting the worst and will soon begin to imagine unfavorable events, and this in turn will attract the necessary resources to bring the bad luck to reality — which then confirms the belief, making it become even stronger.

How about someone who has a black cat in their house? They obviously don't hold that belief and are not subjected to the same outcome. That is why it's important to take notice of whether our beliefs are taking us closer to our dreams or further away from them. Are they positive or negative? I hope that through this book, you can identify any deep-seated beliefs you may have that have hindered your happiness, and then, through practice, change them.

Whether we like it or not, the four laws of success are always at work, aiding or opposing our success. We can either use the laws to help us succeed, or stay ignorant and leave our success to chance. These are universal laws. You can either believe in them or reject them but you cannot wish them away. The laws continue to manifest themselves. Every time you try to disprove them, you end up confirming them. Whether you consciously use them or not, they are always working.

If you are not succeeding, it is because you are not using these laws properly. In this book, I reveal the four laws of success that successful people have used for centuries. I can personally testify to the effectiveness of these powerful laws and how they can shape our destiny, as can the hundreds of people I have coached over the years.

But just knowing these laws is not enough. You need to know how to make them work for you. After all, everyone knew about the laws governing flight, but the Wright brothers made it work for them and changed the course of history.

I hope that by applying these laws in your life you will create the life of your dreams.

Chapter 1
FROM DREAMS TO REALITY: MY JOURNEY

"It is not how much we have, but how much we enjoy, that makes happiness."

— *Charles Spurgeon*

Life can be unpredictable at times. It takes sharp twists and turns quite suddenly and unexpectedly. Right when we feel that we are in total control of our life, we are caught unaware and all of a sudden, life seems to fall apart.

One day, destiny turned the tables on my family and me, and at the very tender age of five, I experienced what the phrase "life falling apart" actually meant. The comfortable life we lived came crumbling down under the force of unfortunate events, leaving us feeling totally powerless.

It was the decade after India achieved its independence. My father had a job in the government, earning a decent salary that provided us with all the luxuries of life. My father was posted in a place called Kalol, near Ahmedabad in Gujarat, India. We lived in a beautiful home. We had servants, cooks, and all the material things one could wish for. I was the youngest amongst four siblings; one brother and two sisters. We all lived a very happy and blessed life, but one day everything was suddenly swept away – my father died of a massive heart attack.

In a flash, everything went upside down in our lives. Thereafter, our lives were in complete disarray. We had to vacate the house we were living in, as it was a government accommodation. My father was the only breadwinner in the family and therefore we did not know how we would continue to survive.

We were a large family and all of us were studying. The expenses were immense, and the pension my mother received was a meager sum. We got another blow when all our relatives deserted us, thinking that we would be a burden on them. We had to move to a small village nearby called Chhatral and my mother could only afford a small room. This room served as a living area, kitchen, and bedroom, and the bathroom facilities were in nature. There was no electricity or running water — luxuries we once had. All that we had become accustomed to while my father was alive was taken away from us within moments.

Up until that point, my mother had never experienced hardships. She came from an affluent family and due to my father's position in the government she was provided with all the luxuries that she had gotten used to. In spite of that, she handled the situation with grace. We were completely uprooted, but my mother was not one to cry over spilled milk. She was an embodiment of strength and took charge of her life, and was determined to educate her four children well so that they could live a better life. In the midst of all the difficulties and chaos my mother had a firm belief that "everything will be fine." I inherited this belief from her.

We were not aware of our father's investments, if any, and were left with very little money. My mother invested that money in land and leased it out for farming. The people of Chhatral, led by Vithhalbhai Patel, came forward and with their help she started a kindergarten and began sewing classes. My mother was an entrepreneur and I attribute my entrepreneurial drive to her.

Along with our schooling my siblings and I started to work. Our job was to remove cotton from cotton buds and earn money in return. Life started to move on.

One day, while studying in the 8th grade, I saw a vendor at school selling candy and snacks to the kids during recess. My entrepreneurial instincts kicked in. I proposed to the principal to let me use an empty storage room in the school for my shop and offered to give a major portion of the profit to the school. He agreed, and I set up shop during recess while the other kids played. By then, I had formed a belief that life was easier with money and because I wanted a better life, I did whatever it took to make money.

Growing up in a small village, my world was small and limited. I knew of nothing else. Jyotiben had just gotten married, and her husband was going to America for his Ph.D. That was the first time I heard about the 'land of opportunity.' He would send us pictures of America that ignited a dream in me, and I knew I wanted to be there.

Once, when I was sitting outside with my mother, I saw a plane fly by. I told her, "One day, I will take you in that plane to America and we will live a phenomenal life." By then I had formed two fundamental beliefs: Firstly, "If I work hard and believe in myself, I can accomplish almost anything," and secondly, "I will go to America and earn a lot of money and live an exceptionally good life." How was I going to achieve that? Well, I was absolutely clueless. I fueled my imagination and began expecting the results as if they were already there.

During my last year in high school our financial situation started to improve. I was still glued to my belief that I would earn a lot of money and create a good life for my family, which became stronger and stronger every passing day. When in college, I decided to become a doctor, solely because doctors made a lot of money. My mother had instilled in us confidence and the belief that we would achieve what we wanted in our lives. Once I made that decision, I began working very hard to achieve that. As a step towards my dream, I started volunteering at a doctor's office, assisting him as a compounder, to get exposure of what it was like to be a doctor.

Sometimes the Universe has its own way of putting you on the right path to manifest your beliefs. I was a bright student and everyone was confident that I would get into medical college. But somehow I did not perform well on the entrance exam and could not gain admission into medicine. I had to continue with pursuing a degree in science with no declaration. I became depressed and saw my dreams shatter before me. It was a direct threat to my belief. My fears started playing on my mind: "If I don't become a doctor, I will not be able to earn good money and will not be able to live the life I've dreamed of."

But my mother consoled me, saying, "Everything happens for a good reason. You may have some other opportunity waiting for you. Don't give up on your dream." She wasn't just saying that to make me feel better — she was speaking from her experience and her belief.

We generally form our beliefs, good and bad, based on the events that occur, people we associate with, and our dreams and goals. Everything seems good when things are going as per our expectations, but even one negative incident has the potential to destroy our positive beliefs. At such times we need someone to be there by our side to tell us, "Hey, everything's going be fine."

I consider myself very fortunate that this role was played by my mother. Whatever I am today, I owe it to her. I realized that as parents, we have a huge responsibility for the beliefs we instill in our children. Children are great observers and they absorb everything happening around them, positive or negative. That assimilation shapes their beliefs and later becomes their reality.

After we got the news that I was not accepted to medical college, our tenant's younger brother, who was a professor at a pharmacy college in Ahmedabad, suggested that I try for pharmacy, which is a related subject. Without really knowing what I was getting into, I decided to take up pharmacy out of desperation. What that meant was that I would have to commit to an extra year to graduate pharmacy school, a decision that was hard to make because that meant one more year of fees.

To make matters worse I flunked my first year and had to stay back, I graduated college two years later than my high school friends, in the year 1976. At the time, it seemed like a huge failure, however had I not failed, I would not have met my best friend in life, Kiran Joshi, and his family. Kiran's father was the Secretary (Chief of Staff) to the Governor of Gujarat, and he became the father figure I so badly missed. I learned many valuable lessons from him, lessons that have made me the man I am today.

After graduating, I got a job in a pharmaceutical company in Valsad and had to move there. During that time America had stopped granting visas to doctors and had opened doors for nurses and pharmacists. This meant that I was one step closer to my dream of moving to America. I applied for the visa but since the American consulate was flooded with applications, they decided to restrict the entry by introducing an English language test for the first time. Accordingly, letters were sent to all the applicants; however, I did not receive it on time due to my relocation to another town for work. By the time it was redirected and received the exam was already over.

Once again I could see my dreams slipping through my hands like sand, but I immediately snapped out of it and told myself, "Whatever happens or doesn't happen in my life is for my good." I went with the letter to the US consulate office and explained the issue. To my utter surprise, he took me in directly for the interview, skipping the exam. I was thrilled to see my belief at work. I realized that had I appeared for the English exam, I would have failed miserably, as having studied in Gujarati, my English was very poor. I ended up getting a visa and started making plans for the US.

I landed in the US in 1978 with $20 in my pocket and two suitcases. I learned of a vacancy for an assistant to the manager in one of the largest pharmacy chain stores in New York. Due to some confusion with the trains, I reached the store three hours late for the interview. I still remember the words of the manager. He said, "If you can't even find the store, how will you find the medicine? Get out of here!" I was fired from the job even before I started. I was jobless again. One of my friends knew of a bank which was looking to hire someone for temporary work as a mail room clerk, so I took the job, as I needed it desperately.

After I started working, the department head and I developed a good rapport and he ended up offering me a full-time position as a computer operator in the newly opened data center in Queens, New York. At this point I had to make a decision: would I continue a career in pharmacy or would I start on a new path in technology? In spite of a lot of resistance from my family and friends, I made one of the most pivotal decisions of my life — I chose to end my pharmacy chapter forever as my instincts told me that technology was the future and I knew that I could become successful in that field. I took up the job and there was no looking back after that. Within 10 years I became a Vice President in the computer department of Citibank.

Behind my success there was lots of hard work and dedication. During those years, I acquired an MBA from Long Island University while continuing to work full-time. While getting my MBA, I married my wife, Mina, who is my greatest asset and biggest support system. Soon after, we were blessed with our first child Kavan.

I was earning pretty well to live the lifestyle I had aspired for, but with little to no time for myself and my family. I hardly met my son. He would be sleeping when I left for work in the morning and was in bed by the time I reached home at night. It hurt me when I could not be there for my family. I started questioning myself, saying, "It's true that I wanted to earn a lot of money, but at what cost?"

Being a family-oriented person, I longed to spend some quality time with my family, I needed to take better care of my health, and I wanted to pursue my own passions. The life I had created for myself was not what I had aimed for. I didn't want to trade my time for money and therefore I began looking for other opportunities.

The law of attraction came into play. Our son Kavan was five years old and my wife Mina was pregnant with our second child, Mona. My friend who worked at the bank with me introduced me to the network marketing concept, which I was able to pursue with my wife Mina as our own business. In the beginning, I would build our business part-time while handling my demanding job. Did I have to work hard and make sacrifices in the beginning? Yes, but my belief that it would work did pay off and Mina and I eventually were able to become full-time entrepreneurs, allowing us to set our own goals and giving us back control over our time.

We were fortunate to meet our mentors and guides Kanti and Lata Gala, and our son Kavan married their daughter Anjali, over 8 years ago.

Money started working for me instead of me toiling hard for it. Our lives changed completely. I could finally spend a lot of quality time with my family, which strengthened our bond. Today, I get to give my undivided attention to our grandson, Nikhil, and our granddaughter, Sia. We are able to travel all over the world and live in our dream home. I got the 'me time' that permitted me to take care of my health and pursue my hobbies. I always wanted to write a book, and I can now take my love for music more seriously by taking vocal classes and giving performances. I am doing what I have always wanted to do and enjoying life to its fullest. What more could anybody ask for?

Now, looking back, I can connect the dots. One incident led to another, and it was so beautifully crafted that it set me on my path in a direction towards my goal, powered by my beliefs. When I look back now, I realize that at times, I was guided by my gut feeling or intuition, while at other times, some things were forced upon me. But eventually, each and every thing that happened directed me towards my ultimate goal, which was to live in America, earn a lot of money, and make money work for me rather than me working for it. I achieved the American dream.

The Universe has its own unique ways of working through you. It speaks to you through your subconscious mind. You need to silence the chatter of your conscious mind, go within, and listen to your subconscious. It will surely guide you towards your destination.

Design your life. Believe in it, imagine it, expect it. Work hard and you will attract it. Be the architect and builder of your own life.

Chapter 2
I WILL BE HAPPY WHEN . . .

"Folks are usually about as happy as they make their minds up to be."
                                           — *Abraham Lincoln*

It was late in the evening and I was still in the office juggling to complete my to-do list for work. Most of my colleagues had left for home, barring a few. My office was on the seventh floor in the Financial District, right by the water, from where we had the most mesmerizing panoramic view of the east river with views of the Brooklyn Bridge and the Manhattan Bridge. The city especially looked its best in the evening with differently colored lights happily dancing through the high-rise buildings.

I was sitting in my private office behind a huge desk. The beige-colored carpet, white walls, and floor-to-ceiling window on my right made my office look very elegant and spacious. It was a busy day and I was still left with a few correspondences to be sent before calling it a day. I looked outside my window, taking a moment to enjoy the outside view, lost in my thoughts.

I was working with a leading Wall Street bank in New York. I had just been promoted to Vice President of the data processing department. It was a great achievement for a person like me who had come from a poor family from a small village in Gujarat, India. Moreover, with this achievement, I was just a few steps away from the goal I had set for myself. I joined the bank as a mail room clerk, as I needed to make some money until I got my license to practice pharmacy. One thing led to another and I never left the bank. And after ten years of tirelessly working there, I had reached a position where I felt I could be financially satisfied.

By that time, Kavan was four years old, and Mina was pregnant with Mona. My routine was always bustling with activities mostly related to my work, which left me with no time for myself and my family. I woke up every morning at 5 a.m. to go to work and came back home late in the evening. When I left in the mornings my son would be sleeping and by the time I came home he'd be fast asleep again. I hardly got to spend time with my son.

I was in a position many people would be envious of. I had earned this through sheer hard work and dedication. However, I was missing out on the most important years of my children's life, nor was I getting time to spend with my wife, and that tore me apart. They deserved more than that from me. I could give them all the luxuries money can buy, but what good was that when my relationship with them would get tarnished in the process? The price I paid for success was at the cost of my family, which was no longer was okay with me.

The chain of thoughts compelled me to introspect. I realized that it had been long since I spent quality time with my family. I was completely neglecting my health. I had no time whatsoever for anything other than work. The questions I had been avoiding to confront began to occupy much of my thinking.

"Was I really happy missing the growing years of my child and the beautiful moments with my wife during her pregnancy?"

"Will all the money I am earning pay for these invaluable moments that I am missing?"

"Am I happy with the way my life is going?"

I was astonished when my inner voice, which I had suppressed over the years, told me I had to redefine what happiness meant to me.

I was so absorbed in my zest to earn money that I never really pondered upon the question, "Am I happy?" I always thought that money would bring happiness. Up until that moment, I had so strongly believed that money can buy all that is needed for a good life. If my philosophy was right, then why couldn't money buy me time? My philosophy that earning a lot of money brings happiness came crashing down with a whirlpool of thoughts. I felt I should be there with my wife for her doctor's visits. I should be there for my little Kavan as his best buddy during his growing up years. As soon as I allowed myself to take down my false pretense of success, a fundamental shift took place within – I realized that I could not be happy and successful in the true sense if others around me were unhappy, especially my family.

I decided to take care of the pending work the next day, and left for home. Mina was shocked to see me come home early that day. I sat down with her to discuss my new revelations. I told her, "Mina, this is not how I want to live my life. I'm OK with making less money if that means spending more time with you and the kids. What is the use of money if I am not by your side when you need me?"

She just held my hand and asked, "What do you plan to do?"

"As long as I am working for someone, all I will be doing is trading my time for money." After a pause, I added, "Well, we need to have a plan B."

I knew I needed to do something, though I was not sure what.

I started going to all kinds of seminars and classes to check out various businesses. I started seriously looking for other opportunities. In the process, I stumbled upon a network marketing business. I was not quite sure if that would work for me. But Mina said, "We have nothing to lose, and what if it works?"

I started thinking sincerely about it and decided to try it. Within five years of working a full-time job at the bank and building a business in my spare time, I was able to gain control over my time and money. I was able to give up my full-time job at the bank in 1994 and get my time back while I made money, too. It's been over 21 years since then and I am enjoying my life and helping others to do the same. Today, without the slightest doubt, I can say that I am a happy and successful man.

Success does not create happiness.

> *"Success comes from knowing that you did your best to become the best that you are capable of becoming."*
> *—John Wooden*

Though the definition of success and happiness differs from person to person, there is a tendency to equate happiness with success. There was a time when I believed that the only way I would be successful is if I acquired a lot of wealth. But during my journey, I realized that only money and material things cannot give us happiness.

Say you have a 2,000 square foot house, and you feel you'd be happier if you had a 5,000 square foot house. Happiness does not come from objects, and therefore your level of happiness won't change with a new house. You may feel excited and joyous for a while, but that will fade away if the source of your happiness does not change. Continuously placing your happiness on external objects will only be good as long as the objects last.

Often people think that once the success is achieved, then happiness will be found. Some people believe that thinking about happiness takes you away from success. These types of thinking show the effect. We often see rich people taking medicines for depression. We see a lack of mental peace in them. The success achieved on the basis of any compromise cannot give you happiness.

Many people, in their rise to success, are so busy running to the top, stepping on their competitors, stepping on their enemies, and saddest of all, stepping on their friends and loved ones, that when they get to the top, they look around and discover that they are extremely lonely and unhappy.

They'll ask me, "Where did I go wrong?"

My answer has always been, "Probably at the beginning."

Many times, people see success in different meanings. People first want to fill the inadequacies of their lives, and so they move in the rat race. Finding more than they need is success for them. But even after achieving the success, when they do not find happiness, they again start looking towards their real needs. You must have seen many examples when people leave everything for their happiness. They try to understand the true meaning of their success. It may happen to you as well. It is therefore better that you know the purpose of your success first. Find out what your success really means for you.

Happiness and success are very subjective terms. Many people often ask me if there is a formula or tool they can use to define their success criteria. I wish I could give them one, but unfortunately, there is none. However, there is a rule of thumb that I have used personally and taught to thousands of people over the past twenty years. Ask yourself the question, "What makes me happy? What do I want that will make me happy?"

Make a detailed list that covers your intentions and goals in:

1. *Health*

2. *Wealth*

3. *Relationships*

4. *Spirituality*

Find out what makes you happy in each area, not just one. Introspection is the first step to finding true happiness and success.

The next step is understanding that real happiness is striking a balance in each of the areas that you defined that works for you. Having said that, you should strive to have enough wealth, good health, strong relationships, and a great spiritual life to be truly happy to the extent where you're not depriving yourself or your family of a good life. Without the self-awareness of where you need to devote more of your attention, success will always be elusive.

It's important to understand this earlier rather than later, because achieving better balance becomes even more difficult with the passage of time. Self-awareness at every stage of your life is vital. One rule I have followed in my life is to avoid extremes.

Don't focus on wealth at the cost of your health, relationships, and spiritual well-being. You cannot ignore money, either, to get the other areas of life to be perfect. If you don't have sufficient income, it will affect your health because worries will increase your stress, which will affect your relationships, too. Money won't necessarily give us happiness, but it will allow us to get more joy from other areas. In short, we have to learn to strike a balance in all four areas of our life to create happiness.

On scale of 1 to 10, if you average 7 across all four categories, that's great. You may not get to 10, but you should always be working towards it. Sometimes, in order to achieve balance, you may need to get out of balance for the time being. For example, while working full-time, I was missing out on quality time with my family. In that regard, I was totally out of balance. I knew that the only way to get back into balance was to find a better source of income.

Once I began my business for achieving better balance, I had to take even more time away from my family, which made it seem even worse at the time. However, I knew that this was only for a short period of time; and within 5 years of starting my business I was able to regain my time a hundredfold. The key here is that sometimes you may need to sacrifice something from certain areas of life to achieve success, but only if it's for a short period of time. I worked very hard for 5 years with little time to spare, but after that I had all the time and money needed to truly enjoy life.

Lastly, and most importantly, understand that for lasting success and happiness you need to ask yourself, "How many people are better off because I am living?" Giving is a crucial element of achieving true happiness. There are many ways to give. It could be through money, your time, or something as simple as a compliment. Remember, if there is an element of giving in everything you do, your happiness will be greatly amplified. There is no greater joy than making a difference in somebody's life. It makes your life worthwhile. It could be in the form of being kind, expressing gratitude, helping someone in need, and so on.

IN A NUTSHELL

- *Success is not necessarily happiness. Success does not create happiness.*

- *Happy people are successful, but successful people may or may not be happy.*

- *Real happiness is achieved when you strike a balance in each of the areas of your life. You cannot be happy in one area of your life at the cost of other areas. You have to be happy in all areas of your life such as health, wealth creation, relationships, and spiritual well-being.*

- *True happiness is measured by how many people are better off because you lived.*

- *Happiness is a choice. Choose to be happy.*

Chapter 3
HOW THE MIND WORKS

"If you correct your mind, the rest of your life will fall into place."

— *Lao Tzu*

A lot has been said about the mind and its powers by sages and philosophers across time. Many stories can be found on how the power of the mind has taken individuals to new horizons.

Though we may not be fully aware of it, we can get exactly what we want by using the power of our mind. However, to use this power effectively we have to understand how our mind works.

For all practical purposes, let's say that our mind is divided into two parts, the conscious and the subconscious. There are a few experts who further divide the subconscious into two parts, the subconscious and the unconscious. But for our discussion we will only discuss the conscious and subconscious minds.

What are the conscious and subconscious minds and how do they function together?

Our conscious mind is like the manager of a department who makes decisions and delegates tasks to staff members in his/her team. Our subconscious mind, in this case, is made of the people in the department who carry out the orders and produce results. One interesting thing to note here is that the subconscious has to obey the orders given to it by the conscious mind. It does not have the power to reject or judge the orders given.

The conscious mind receives input and ideas, and communicates with the outside world using the five senses. If it chooses to, it will send this information to the subconscious for processing. It also stores short-term memories such as what you just had for lunch, or the name of someone who you just met.

Our conscious mind takes charge when we do something for the first time. First we do it consciously, then semi-consciously, and with enough repetition we do it subconsciously. Remember how you learned to ride a bike, swim, or drive a car? The first time you got on a bike, you were completely conscious of the entire process. As you rode that bike more often, you were able to ride with more ease, but there may have been some hesitation. It is not until riding became second nature to you that you became confident about it and let any conscious control go. We hesitate when we do anything consciously, but when we do it subconsciously it is done with ease.

The subconscious mind is the storehouse of all our memories; even those we may have forgotten consciously. It remembers what you ate a few months ago, or the name of a person you met five years ago. It also stores all the beliefs, emotions, and feelings that are attached to your past experiences. This information is presented to the subconscious mind through our conscious mind. When the conscious mind needs it, it will ask for that information from the subconscious. It is from these memories and experiences that our current beliefs are formed. Information that is stored in our subconscious mind affects our behavior and actions. The subconscious mind is certainly an active and smart part of the brain. If you learn how to make it work for you, it can do wonders in your life.

Our subconscious mind is working 24/7. On the other hand, the conscious mind needs rest. When the conscious mind is resting, the subconscious mind takes charge. The conscious mind slows down or completely shuts down, and the subconscious mind takes over while we are sleeping, just before we fall asleep, and just before we fully wake up. This is the best time for auto-suggestions and visualization. It is easier to communicate to the subconscious mind during that time, because when the conscious mind is at complete rest, access to the subconscious mind is restricted.

Accessing it can also be done through meditation. When you quiet your mind using meditation techniques, you are consciously and unconsciously reprogramming your mind. There are various techniques that you can apply during meditation, which could involve incorporating visualization and imagination as a point of focus for whatever belief you want your subconscious mind to develop. This will be discussed in greater detail later on in the book.

Another analogy to explain this concept is this. Think of your mind as a computer. A computer consists of the hard drive, input devices (such as a keyboard, optical devices, or a microphone), RAM (random access memory), the central processing unit (CPU), and output devices (such as a monitor, speakers, or a printer).

Our conscious mind serves as an input device. Data is entered through the keyboard and results are shown on the monitor. Input devices are also used to create programs, which are stored on the hard drive. It also serves as the RAM in our computer. RAM is the place in a computer where programs and data that are currently in use or frequently used, are kept for quick access.

Our subconscious mind is like the CPU and hard drive. It processes the input data and creates results based on the programs that were previously installed — created by the conscious mind. It is the long-term storage place for all our memories, beliefs, and programs that have been installed since we were born. The subconscious mind is the most powerful processing system ever known.

Two identical computers can produce different results from the same input based on which programs are running. It is the underlying program that determines the outcome, not the computer hardware or input. If we don't like the results that we are getting, we may have to modify the input, or if the input is correct, than we may need to change the program. An input of 2 and 2 into a computer may result in an answer of 0 or 4. Answer depends entirely on whether the program is that of subtraction, multiplication, or addition.

Understand that our subconscious mind is not in charge. Our conscious mind gives the directions based on stored programming. The subconscious will only deliver the emotions and feelings of what we continuously think about. If we don't like the result, we have to change things at a conscious level. Now, I am not saying that it is as easy as changing what you think of in one moment and that your entire life will be changed. In most cases, your current programs have been running for so long and cannot be changed instantaneously.

If you want to effect change in your life, then you will have to work on rewriting your programs that are held in the subconscious mind. There are specialized ways to make that happen, such as visualization and use of affirmations, which will change your belief system. The place to start doing that is in the conscious mind, by continuously being in charge of your own thoughts through affirmations, directing our focus and using visualization. This will be discussed further in the book.

If you really want to bring about a positive change in your life, you need to work on rewriting your programs — that is, beliefs that are seated in the subconscious mind. The work on this starts at the conscious level. This can be achieved by continuously being in charge of your own thoughts through affirmations, directing your focus, and using visualization.

We can influence the programs that run in the background of our subconscious mind. If we do this with consistent and persistent effort, our subconscious belief system will be reprogrammed and we will experience miraculous changes in our life. If we use our subconscious mind effectively and constructively, we can lead a healthy and happy life.

That being said, the subconscious mind can't do magic. Some people think that they can use their subconscious mind to change their financial situation while being careless about money, but it cannot be done, because the message you are sending to the subconscious in this case is that you do not want money.

The good news is that it can be easily reprogrammed. Every night before you go to bed, make requests to your subconscious mind. It can be anything relating to your personal life or career. Once you have made requests, you have to repeatedly imagine yourself enjoying the life that you want. Keep practicing it until your imagination turns into reality. It is also important to think about the joy that you will experience when your dream become a reality. Use affirmations to go along with your visualizations and slowly you will begin to manifest your dreams. Always trust your subconscious mind's ability to make it happen.

IN A NUTSHELL

- *The conscious mind makes decisions about what you want using the information given to it using the five senses. The conscious mind determines what is good and bad, right and wrong. It is the thinking mind. It will accept or reject ideas based on the stored data and program.*

- *Our subconscious mind is our servant. It cannot make decisions on its own. It cannot differentiate right from wrong, good from bad, positive from negative, or a good feeling from a bad feeling. It can only act upon what the conscious mind wants.*

- *Our subconscious mind has unlimited resources but no authority; while our conscious mind has limited information but it is the master. The subconscious mind has to receive requests and approval from the conscious mind to produce what we want.*

- *Don't use your conscious mind to figure out how you will get what you want. It is not capable of doing that, leave that up to your subconscious mind. Every time you think about 'how,' you will create doubts and fear. When you create feelings of doubt and fear, the subconscious becomes confused and will pay attention to those feelings.*

- *Applying how the conscious and subconscious mind works will allow you to write a new script of a life of your choice.*

SECTION I

LAW OF BELIEF

Chapter 4
WE ARE WHAT WE BELIEVE

"We often become what we believe ourselves to be. If I believe I cannot do something, it makes me incapable of doing it. When I believe I can, I acquire the ability to do it, even if I didn't have it in the beginning."
— *Mahatma Gandhi*

It was 18 June, 2004. Mina and I were in Dallas, Texas for a motivational speaking engagement. We were excited to address about five thousand people who were eagerly waiting to listen to us. The talk was to start at 10 p.m., and as we were readying ourselves to step on to the podium to face the enthusiastic crowd, my phone rang.

It was our neighbor, Kanti. He informed me that our house was on fire and the firefighters were trying very hard to control it. Then, hesitantly, he explained that the situation was beginning to go out of control.

I could catch the worried tone in his voice and read between the lines, and I understood that not much would remain after the fire died down. All that concerned me at that moment was the safety of our children, and fortunately we were informed that they were fine.

It was indeed shocking news, but something from within told me, "Look, you are fifteen hundred miles away from home. Is there any way you can help the situation? The firefighters are already doing their job. So relax!" I realized there was nothing I could do at that point in time other than staying calm.

I informed a few friends who were there with us; we cheered ourselves up and went up on stage to give our talk. The talk concluded with a huge round of applause. When we came off the stage, one of our friends who was backstage and knew about this incident went up and said, "Can any of you believe that while Kulin and Mina were talking to you, their house in New Jersey was on fire, and that they got the news just before coming on stage to speak?" Nobody could believe it. People were stunned at how we could handle such news and still keep our cool.

From a very early stage of my childhood, a strong belief was instilled in me by my mother that whatever happens always happens for a good reason. We should not worry about the things that are not in our control. It is best to leave it to God. That belief has carried into everything that I do today and has served as a guide through all the situations in my life.

The next day, when we came back to New Jersey, the sight was distressing. Everything had been devastated by the fire. What Mina and I had so lovingly built together was reduced to ashes. But it didn't really bother us that much because we knew we had everything we needed in each other. As long as we were together nothing was lost that could not be replaced. Material things are transient, but relationships are not.

When we met with the firefighters to thank them for their effort, they told us how impressed they were with our children and the way we had raised them. They explained how in most situations like this, they have to deal more with the panic of family members than the fire itself. In our case, they were pleasantly surprised when our kids asked if they could do anything to help instead. We were proud of our children and thanked God that we were able to transfer the same belief to them. We knew and believed everything would work out for the best, and it did. A few years have passed since the fire, and today we have a bigger house with more facilities and luxuries than the one we had before.

This is a small example of how a positive belief can help us get through difficult situations in life and eventually lead to something much more beautiful than expected.

What is a belief?

A belief is an assumption we make in the form of a powerful thought, fueled by the conviction that it is true, which later turns it into reality. This thought could be a positive thought or a negative one, which then becomes the governing factor for our life. It defines how we think, act, and achieve.

How are our beliefs formed?

The foundation for beliefs are laid out at a very young age. Our beliefs depend upon the way we perceive the world through our sense organs. Our brain starts processing what we see, feel, and hear. It is a certain opinion we form about ourselves or about the things and people around us, influenced by our own experiences and that of people around us. If we are told certain things about ourselves and about the world which we start accepting, a belief is created. A belief that we assimilate may or may not be true. It is just a perception influenced by everything around us.

Well, if the beliefs are positive, there is no harm. Positive beliefs help us achieve our dreams. But if the beliefs are negative, they can be destructive. My friend had a long-standing dream of starting his own business. His father decided to support him and invested all of his savings in helping his son start a business. Despite all his hard work, the business was an abysmal failure and within a couple of years, he went bankrupt. He had to sell his house to pay the debts.

However, this episode morally pulled him down and he started believing that he could no longer succeed in business. Although he had a supportive family and they tried to encourage him, the belief he formed about himself that he was not good in business stopped him from taking any steps for improving the situation. Success and failure are part of the game, but forming a belief about the same can completely paralyze your life. This is how detrimental a negative belief you form about yourself can be.

Suppose as a child you mess up something, and after this happens a few times, you are told "you always mess things up" or "you are good for nothing," you'll start believing it, especially if it comes from someone close to you. Or if as a child you fail while doing something and this repeats quite a few times, you will grow in life believing that you are a loser and thus will not be able to achieve anything worthwhile. Also, many believe that you cannot have money and health at the same time, because you need to work really hard to make money, and that affects your health. Of course, if you believe it to be true, then you will accept poor health as a trade-off for having more money. That expectation will soon translate into reality, because whatever we think, we condition our mind to believe.

Have you ever been to a circus? If you have, you would have seen that the elephant is tied to a small pole with a rope. And the interesting part is that the elephant does not even move. It is so obedient that it does not even break from the pole despite its enormous strength and mass. The actual reason is something else. When the elephant is very young, it is tied to the pole in the same way. Naturally, it doesn't like that and tries to escape, but at that time, the rope and the pole are too strong for it. So the elephant eventually gives up and starts believing that how ever much it tries, it will not be able to break the rope and get set free. In the process, the elephant totally forgets its inherent strength and power. The elephant is conditioned to believe that way.

The negative beliefs formed by us about ourselves act as a barrier in achieving what we otherwise could. The elephant in the story above may not have the intelligence to understand that when it grows up, but we humans do.

It is important to realize that your negative beliefs will limit you from achieving what you wish to achieve. You may want a 5,000 square foot house or better health, but if you believe that you won't be able to get it, then the chances are that you never will get it. Whatever you want, you won't get unless your beliefs match your desires.

Psychologists argue that each one of us has a set of beliefs that shape our goals, expectations, and habits that then mold our personality and determine our actions and achievements. Your current belief system is created based on everything good or bad that has happened to you in the past and everything that will happen to you in the future. Your response to the situations contributes to the formation of your beliefs.

The worries and anxieties about the future may also give birth to certain beliefs. These beliefs may just be based on the speculations about the future. For example, you may want a few million dollars, but you may think, "How will I get few million dollars when today I am barely earning a few hundred dollars?" This doubt, if entertained, grows in your mind in the form of a belief – "I can never be rich."

If our life is defined by the beliefs we nurture, then changing our beliefs can also change our life. The negative beliefs can be dislodged and replaced by positive ones. There is a growing body of research which shows that we can change our belief systems to achieve whatever we want in life.

In a rigorous study of college students at a university, students in the experimental group were shown a film that highlighted how the brain is capable of making new connections throughout life, and how it grows in response to intellectual challenges. They also wrote a letter to struggling younger students emphasizing that the brain is malleable and that intelligence expands with hard work.

At the end of that semester, the college students who had learned about the brain's ability to grow and adapt showed greater value for academics, took more joy in their academic work, and achieved higher grade point averages when compared to a control group that had not learned about the brain's abilities. (Aronson, Fried, and Good, 2002)

Most of us believe that intellect is static, that you are either born with it or not. This results in most people accepting that they have limited intelligence and act accordingly, thus limiting their achievements. But knowing that the brain could continue to grow and become better with studying allowed these students to replace the belief about their static intellect with a new one that says that if they worked hard, they would become intelligent and would earn better grades. Armed with a new belief, the students showed considerable improvement.

Beliefs also come in the form of superstitions or lucky charms. In many parts of India, if you boil milk and it spills over, it is considered a bad omen — a sign that something bad is going to happen. Some years ago, I was at a friend's house for a new housewarming event and I saw a pot of boiling milk about to spill over. My instinctive reaction was to ask someone to switch off the stove, but the host said they intended for it to spill over because it brought good luck. It surprised me that while being part of the same culture, what brought good luck to one brought bad luck to the other. It is only the belief that brings good luck or bad luck, not the milk.

When I was growing up in India, I had a friend who believed that he had to see a cow before leaving his house for an important event such as going for an exam, and he would ask me to secure a cow in front of his house before he left. While this may sound ridiculous, his belief was so strong that it did in fact bring him good luck. I wonder what would have happened if he had to stay in the US, where seeing a cow on the road would be next to impossible unless he lived on a farm.

Astrology is quite prevalent in many parts of India. Though it may have a scientific base attached to it, given the time we are living in, some people find it ridiculous to follow. People generally go to astrologers when they are passing through a bad phase in life and are not able to see any good ahead. The prediction made by the astrologer that something good will happen in the future gives the person hope, and he forms a belief that since the astrologer has affirmed that something good will happen, it will happen. This positive belief then attracts positive events in his life.

All of us believe that in order to lose weight, we need to exercise and eat right. This is born out of a belief that the body responds to these factors in a mechanical way – if we exercise we will burn energy, and if we eat right we will accumulate less weight.

I know of a woman who was overweight and was trying very hard to lose weight. She followed a strict exercise regime, went on a hardcore diet, and did everything that could possibly be done to slim down. But somewhere in her mind, she always thought and believed that she would not lose weight. She always said, "It is so difficult for me to lose a significant amount of weight." Slowly, this became her affirmation which she repeated several times during the day. The result was that she barely lost weight despite all efforts and she finally gave up.

In another case, there was a young girl who formed a belief that the more junk food she ate, the more weight she would lose. And she actually started shedding a few pounds. While I certainly do not advocate this, as eating excessive amounts of junk food will hamper our health later on, what I am trying to emphasize here is that a belief — positive or negative — will influence the outcome.

Many times we may have the right beliefs but how we apply them can make all the difference. Alia Crum and Ellen Langer, from the Harvard University Department of Psychology, conducted a study of 84 hotel room attendants in seven hotels to find out how it worked.

A room attendant cleans, on average, 15 rooms per day with each room taking between 20 to 30 minutes to clean. It is physically intensive work and it meets the US Surgeon General's recommendation of at least 30 minutes of physical exercise per day for a healthy lifestyle. However, the researchers found that the attendants did not look at their work as exercise and believed that they did not get any exercise at all. As in any scientific experiment, the attendants were separated into two groups – the informed, or treatment, group, and the control group.

Attendants in the informed group were told that their work met the Surgeon General's recommendations for an active lifestyle and were provided specific examples of why their work qualified as exercise. Those in the control group were not told anything. After just four weeks, the attendants in the treatment group showed a decrease in weight, blood pressure, body fat, waist-to-hip ratio, and body mass index. The attendants in the control group, however, did not show any improvement in these parameters.

What happened?

Equipped with the information that their work itself was exercise, the attendants now believed that they were living a healthy lifestyle. They started to expect to lose weight and become healthy. The new belief triggered an expectation that brought about the manifestation of the desired result.

It happened due to a change in belief!

If there is one thing I would want you to take away from this book, it's the knowledge that you have the power to change your belief system. With the right beliefs, nothing is impossible to achieve. Therefore, if there is one thing you wish to change in yourself, start working on your beliefs.

IN A NUTSHELL

- *A belief is an assumption we make in the form of a powerful thought, fueled by the conviction that it is true, which later turns into a reality.*

- *Whatever is in our belief system, whether positive or negative, becomes our reality.*

- *Positive beliefs help us achieve our dreams. But negative beliefs can sabotage our efforts.*

- *Many times we may have the right beliefs, but how we apply them can make all the difference.*

- *Your current reality or your current life is a result of your belief system. You have the power to change your belief system. With the right beliefs, nothing is impossible to achieve.*

Chapter 5
MY BELIEF SYSTEM

"For those who believe, no proof is necessary. For those who don't believe, no proof is possible."
— *Stuart Chase*

Our belief systems are formed since a very young age, sometimes without us really being conscious about them. These belief systems are generally a result of the circumstances we are in and the situations that we go through. The same happened with me after my father's death. I could not see the hardships my mother went through to provide us with the basic necessities of life. That was the time a belief was planted in my mind that one needs to earn a lot of money to lead a comfortable life.

After that, I was burning the midnight oil, studying under the kerosene lamp and street lights, as we had no electricity in our home. Having seen the tough times, my desire and determination to become rich increased with time. But the Universe was continuously working behind my back and had planned something else for me to help me become rich. After my schooling, I could not get an admission into medical school and therefore had to settle for pharmacy as a second choice. Well, my intention was still very clear: I wanted to become successful. Eventually it did happen. Because I took up pharmacy, I could get an easy entry into the US. I got a decently paying job initially which ultimately led me to the life of my dreams, where I did not have to work for money.

What I would like to emphasize here is that though I came from a poor background, my belief that I would become successful helped me reach where I am today. Had I got entangled in the negative belief that "Oh, I am poor. How can I even dream of becoming successful?" I would probably still be in some job with a meager salary in my hometown.

Each one of us creates our own belief system which makes or breaks us.

A good way to judge whether or not you need to change your current beliefs, or adopt new ones, is to monitor your daily emotions. You won't always have positive emotions, but if the majority of your emotions are positive during the day, you will be happy. Your emotions are a reflection of your core beliefs. Most people believe that they have to control their thoughts in order to be happy, but your thoughts come from your core beliefs, so in order to have positive emotions and be happy, you should look at your core beliefs.

My Belief System

I have listed some of my core positive beliefs which I have acquired over time to help you in creating new, positive beliefs for yourself. You don't have to use them word-for-word as what you are seeking in life may be different from what I am. I have mentioned them to illustrate what a positive belief should include. Feel free to create your own or to adopt one of these.

The desire for money is not good or bad. It's how you earn and spend the money that makes it good or bad.

I used to have the negative belief that money is bad. If you have this belief, you will struggle to make ends meet, like I did. But I realized that if you earn your money by doing the right things, by helping people, then that is good money. The better you do, the more money you'll make. You will face many challenges in meeting your financial needs if you believe that money is bad or hard to earn.

My negative belief around money came from accepting word as fact from authoritative figures in my life, which at the times I didn't see as being negative. I later realized that this belief was holding me back from my dream of becoming financially independent.

Always remember that money is the byproduct of your service to another human being. Money will come to you when you serve others, directly or indirectly, because of the blessings that you receive through your act of kindness. Similarly, how you spend the money is also important. If your money is going towards a wrong cause or bad habits, then it is bad money.

Many people believe that desire for money is bad, even sinful. But if I don't have desires, then I won't have the motivation to do anything worthwhile which would help others.

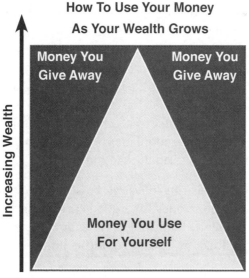

How To Use Your Money As Your Wealth Grows

Money You Give Away

Money You Give Away

Increasing Wealth

Money You Use For Yourself

Square Represents Your Total Income

Different people see money in different perspectives. But the truth is that money is a way of fulfilling the needs. If you are able to fulfill your own needs, you are also able to fulfill the needs of others. If you pay attention to the given picture, you will find that in the beginning, first you have to fulfill your needs. And the entire part of the money is spent only on this. But as you move up in the level of earning, you have more money than your needs, and then you can think about other things.

You are able to give something to your society. You can fulfill all the desires. It is never wrong to have desires. But to choose the wrong path to fulfill it, is wrong.

If I say that my desire is to own a private jet, many people may call it excessive. They might question that desire, saying that a lot of people don't even have a car. My answer is simple – there are people who don't even have a bicycle, and so desiring a car is bad if seen from that point of view.

You see where I'm going with this — pretty soon, every desire will become bad. No one will have any motivation to do anything, and all activities will come to a stop. However, if I become too attached to the idea of owning a plane, then I'll resort to anything to fulfill it, even if it means stealing. What starts as a simple desire becomes harmful because our intentions are misaligned, not because of the desire itself. For this reason, most people stop having any desires at all. They are afraid that if they get too attached to it and can't succeed in earning money honestly, they will resort to harmful activity. To avoid this they stop desiring more money and in turn do not utilize their God-given talents and abilities to the fullest.

Therefore, if I stop desiring physical possessions or having the desire to give away my money for a good cause, then I won't have much need for money. If I don't need more money, then I will stop doing anything productive, because doing so brings in money that

I feel is bad. Effectively, I stop working, I have no motivation, and I am wasting away my skills and expertise. I stop helping people.

My purpose for sharing my thoughts on desire and money is to create the right awareness. I want you to dream big and have lots of desires, because it will fully utilize your talents and abilities to create wealth and abundance, which in turn will help lots of people, and can, when spent for a good reason, create a healthy economy. If not, so much talent would go to waste, which could otherwise be channeled to create a better future for you and everyone around you.

I deserve good health

I believe I deserve good health. If I don't, then I become prone to developing bad habits such as poor nutrition, lack of exercise, a stressful lifestyle, smoking, and excessive drinking. In fact, there was a time when I did not value my health. I smoked, chewed tobacco, didn't exercise, and ate very unhealthily. I remember when Mina would make me salad, I'd tell her that that was meant for animals and I told her to give me real food.

The day I started believing my health needed to be a priority, I quit all those bad habits. It wasn't easy and it required a tremendous amount of self-discipline, but my belief in good health was so strong that today I can say I am truly living the healthiest of lives.

Healthy diet is very important. But, just changing the diet cannot guarantee a good health. You need to have a good mind as well. A pure mind can never take impure food. You have to create a belief within yourself.

You need to believe that you have time to work out. You have to believe that you have healthy eating habits.

This is not new to most people. Everyone has this knowledge but most people fail to implement it. A common reason for not exercising is a lack of time. But let's say this becomes a requirement for earning your paycheck. Would you find the time? I am sure you would, and just where did that time come from?

This will only last as long as the requirement is there, but if you do it by yourself, it will last a lifetime. Most of us are used to being disciplined by others instead of utilizing self-discipline. I am so glad that I did. When you value something, you will always find a way to do it.

Unfortunately, some people only make changes when they find out from their doctor that they have developed some kind of lifestyle disease such as cancer, diabetes, or cardiovascular disease. In most cases, it is too late. I believe it is wise to dig a well before you need water.

I believe I am good with people

From very early in my life, I developed a strong belief that I would like to help people. In order to accomplish that, I realized that I needed to be good with other people. I also realized that I would need other people to succeed at anything worthwhile. Love and support from others is the greatest asset one can acquire, which will help you succeed in all your endeavors. Life is not an individual sport, it is a team effort. Your success depends on others.

I had to develop a self-belief saying that "I am good with people" in order to get help from others. The reason for feeling that I am not good with people is linked to a low self-image. I had to learn to like myself in order to like others. Self-love is important — if you don't love yourself, you can't love anybody else. If I had believed that I was not good with people, then I would not have made an effort to include people in my life. Without others, I would have not succeeded in my journey as well. I believe that I have a healthy self-image, which has enabled me to connect with others well. I believe that I love everybody and that everybody loves me.

Always do unto others as you would want them to do unto you

If I want people to love, respect, and help me, then that is exactly what I should do to others.

I was told while growing up that we should always speak the truth. However, sometimes we face a dilemma. What I have learned from studying religious books is that we should speak the truth as long as it benefits others and does not offend anyone without good reason.

For example, I knock on your door and tell you that some crooks are chasing me and to please let me hide in your house. You let me in. Then the crooks arrive looking for me. You have two options – tell the truth, saying that I am hiding in there, or not tell the truth and save me. But before you answer that, let me turn things around a bit and imagine it is not me hiding in your house but you hiding in mine. What would you want me to tell the bad guys? You would want me to lie to protect you, wouldn't you? Then why should you do any different to me?

Always use this test when in doubt:

Whatever I want other people to do to me are good things to do.

Telling the truth should help others but not hurt others. Is killing somebody good or bad?

It depends. If I kill somebody to rob him, it is bad. But if I am a soldier at war, killing the enemy is good because it helps save my countrymen. Spy agencies routinely steal information to help protect their country. Most of us accept and even encourage it because it helps protect us. But if someone steals the same information to defraud others, it is bad.

The trouble with expecting others not to steal, always tell the truth, and so on is that when we are in the same boat as them, we make justifications for doing just the opposite.

My favorite example is of a couple fighting over whether or not to keep the maid. The wife wants to fire the maid because she is stealing towels. The husband thinks they should keep her because she is doing a good job and it is hard to find a good cleaning crew. The husband asks her, "Which towels are the maid stealing?" The wife says, "The one that we got from the hotel." When the couple took the towels from the hotel, they did not see it as stealing, but when the maid did, it was.

Most people usually don't break big moral values. In my training sessions, I ask people if an elephant has ever bitten them. The answer is a resounding no. But when I ask them whether a mosquito has ever bitten them, the answer is always yes.

The point I am trying to make is that we need to value our values; otherwise, those values will lose their value.

The bottom line is that you have to respect others equally irrespective of their background and beliefs. You may think someone has the wrong beliefs, but also recognize that he probably thinks the same way about you. Sometimes, we take morals and truthfulness verbatim. But we have to see how the moral or the truth is being applied and how it impacts others.

Everything that is happening is happening for a good reason

When I was 10 years old, my mother told me a story that resonated very deeply with me. It has helped me get through many hard times in my life. The story goes like this:

There was a king who was very fond of hunting and used to go on hunts often. Once, when out hunting, he was bitten by a poisonous snake on his toe. The doctor who was part of his entourage took an instant decision and cut off his toe to save his life. When the king realized that he lost his toe, he got angry and the doctor was sentenced to prison for life. Later, when the king recovered from the wound, he started hunting again. This time, while hunting, he got lost and was separated from his entourage.

He ended up at a place where the local tribe was performing a yagna. In Hinduism, a yagna is a ritual of offerings accompanied by chanting mantras and offering sacrifices. An essential element is the ritual fire, into which offerings are poured. Everything that is offered into the fire is believed to reach God. When they saw the King they were very happy that they would be able to offer the best sacrifice to their God.

Before offering the sacrifice, however, they had to give him a bath, during which they found that the king was missing a toe, meaning they would not be able to use him as a sacrifice as he was imperfect. A sacrifice has to be perfect, and so they had to let him go. He left very happy and was able to reunite with his entourage. He thanked God for saving his life but was even more grateful for his lost toe. If he had known that losing his toe was a part of the bigger plan of saving his life, he would have thanked God the day he lost his toe.

The moral of the story is that whatever happens, happens for the best and is part of a bigger plan. Sometimes, we are unable to make sense of the situations in our life, especially when they are less than positive, but you should know that it is only making way for something even grander. God may put you through a smaller problem to save you from a bigger one. Remember this story every time you think, "Why is this happening to me?"

Believing is seeing

Most people say that seeing is believing, but I choose to believe that believing is seeing. You have to start believing in the end results and ignore what is your reality. Believing in the unseen, no matter what it is, is part of getting to a new level in your life.

I believe that there is always a choice

Everything we want is always just one choice away. Please do not get stuck by the confines of your fears. I believed that I had the power to choose a new belief and in doing that, I could change my reality. I chose to believe and that changed everything for me.

Obstacles and struggles are part of the process

I realized very early in my life that everything that I was going through was preparing me for what I had asked for. All that I was experiencing was part of a bigger plan. Later in life when all the pieces of the puzzle joined together, the picture became clear. I realized that all struggles and obstacles were part of the overall plan. I had to surrender to the Universe and accept the good and the bad. I can only control my thoughts and actions, and leave the outcome to God and accept whatever results I get in return with the same attitude of gratitude.

I urge you to consciously look into your beliefs, evaluate them, and change the negative beliefs into positive ones. Once you do that, there is nothing in this world that can stop you from reaching your highest potential.

IN A NUTSHELL

- *Each one of us creates our own core beliefs which make or break us.*

- *Whatever your life is today is nothing but a sum total of your core beliefs, positive and negative.*

- *Our core beliefs are the very essence of how we see ourselves, other people, the world, and the future.*

- *List all your core beliefs and change those which are toxic.*

- *Your emotions are a reflection of your core beliefs. If you want happiness, do not try to control your thoughts. Instead, change your core beliefs.*

Chapter 6
CREATE THE LIFE OF YOUR DREAMS

"There are those who say that seeing is believing. I am telling you that believing is seeing."
— *Neale Donald Walsch*

We all have dreams about achieving success, fulfilling our desires, reaching the top. Tragically though, most dreams never become reality. Let's say that you have the thought, "I wish to become more successful." As soon as that pops into your mind, several other thoughts will also pop up in your mind, telling you how difficult it is. Then it indeed becomes difficult to do it. And the desire just remains a desire.

But if you take a closer look at the thought pattern that emerges against the desire, you will realize that they are emerging out of the negative beliefs you have developed along your life. To be successful in life and to achieve your dreams, it is extremely important to replace the negative beliefs with positive ones.

Here is a seven-step process to help you change your negative beliefs.

1. Recognize and accept the fact that you have some negative beliefs which are limiting you.

This first step in resolving any problem is to recognize that there is a problem. Alcohol addicts cannot be counseled and taken off alcohol till they realize they are addicts. Without accepting the existence of the problem, no solution will ever work because there will be no buy-in or commitment.

People ignore this fact that everything we say has an effect on our lives. We cannot find anything until we want it. In the same way, we can achieve everything we want. Whatever we can think, we can achieve.

I was helping a friend in his business who wanted to be financially successful. One day, we were driving together when we saw a beautiful home. He looked at it and said, "Man, I can never have a house like this!"

I asked him, "What did you just say?" and he repeated the sentence. I said, "That means you really do not want your business to succeed!"

Clearly, his belief system underlying that statement was stopping him from becoming successful. He was working very hard but was not succeeding because he did not expect to succeed. When I pointed out the conflict between what he said and what his thoughts were, he realized that he was creating negative affirmations with his words. He had conceived of being successful but did not believe in it. It was only after he recognized this that he was able to make the necessary changes.

2. Evaluate your existing beliefs and see which ones are working for you. Stick with those beliefs and continue to strengthen them.

Gratitude is a powerful way to strengthen your current positive beliefs. These are the beliefs that have brought all the good things in your life. Maybe you have high self-esteem as a result of a positive belief about your personality. A high self-esteem has enabled you to interact with others in a confident, assured manner which has helped you get that great job or impress someone.

Use gratitude to build positive affirmations about these beliefs. I believe gratitude will make a huge difference in your life. I practice gratitude in my life every day. For example, I like to say:

"Thank you for all the good health, wealth, and happiness I have received in my life. Thank you for abundantly blessing me with all the right qualities to help me fulfill all my needs and desires."

Make a list of all that you are grateful for – good health, great family, your friends, the opportunities you have had in your life. Express gratitude for the opportunity to serve other human beings and for all that makes your life great.

3. Use positive affirmations to replace your negative beliefs with positive ones.

This book is not about affirmations, but I think some information will be helpful for those unfamiliar with it. What we speak has a tremendous impact on us. The words we speak form our belief system. Positive affirmations build our lives, while negative affirmations destroy it. Take a moment and think about whether you use any of these negative affirmations:

- I will never have any money
- I can't afford this
- It is wise to save for a rainy day
- Rich people are greedy
- Money is hard to make
- It takes money to make money
- Money is not everything
- I am not good enough
- I don't deserve it

- Success is difficult
- I don't have what it takes to succeed
- I don't have enough time to do what I need to do
- I am not very good at this
- I worry a lot
- I can't quit smoking/alcohol/drugs
- I can't lose weight no matter what I do
- I don't have time to work out
- I always get sick around this time of the year
- I have a poor memory
- I cannot remember anyone's name
- I just don't get along with them
- Nobody likes me
- I am not that important
- I am not perfect
- Nobody is perfect

The list goes on and on. You can even add a few of your own to this list.

If you say, "Why does nothing good ever happen to me?" your subconscious mind will react to this by bringing more bad things to you. That's what you've asked the subconscious for and that's what you will get in abundance.

But if you say, "All good things happens to me all the time," your subconscious mind will bring more good things to you, because that's what you've asked the subconscious for and so that's what you will get in abundance.

These negative affirmations show how we program our belief systems. Our subconscious is compelled to carry out these negative affirmations, which then reflect in our lives — lack of money, poor relationships, obesity, and poor health. Be aware of every negative statement and turn them around.

Every time you speak a negative statement, change it into a positive one and repeat it. Next time, make sure you use the positive statement instead.

For example, instead of saying "I don't have enough money," you can say, "I get money whenever I need it." Instead of saying, "Making money is difficult," say, "Making money is easy. Money flows to me easily." Get the picture?

If you find yourself repeating a negative statement, write it down in your diary or on a white board. Then strike it out and write the positive version in its place. Repeat it a few times. The picture of you striking out the negative and replacing it with positive is a very powerful visual tool that stays in your subconscious for a long time. Every time you are about to say the negative, the subconscious will replay the scene and remind your conscious mind to say the positive version. It will take time to develop and use positive affirmations repeatedly till your subconscious starts believing it.

When we say an affirmation, you are sending pictures to your subconscious. That is why it is important to think of images that relate to it positively so you can transfer the right images to your subconscious.

Here are a few simple rules for using positive affirmations:

- Always use the present tense. Otherwise your dreams will never make it out of the future and into your present reality! Example: "I make $100,000 a year," or "I weigh 150 pounds," NOT "I want to (or I will) make $100,000 a year," or "I want to (or I will) weigh 150 pounds."

- Always state what you want, NOT what you do not want. Example: "I make $100,000 a year," or "I weigh 150 pounds," NOT "I don't want to be poor," or "I don't want to gain more weight." Focus on what you want. State what you want not from a place of lack, but from a place of already having it (after all, if it exists in your mind, it already exists for you — and imprinting that belief into your subconscious will help make your idea a reality).

- Make your affirmations short and to the point so you can easily remember and repeat them every day.

- Create them in a way that is easy to speak — in your own voice. For example, "There are abundant prospects in every area of my life," is kind of difficult to say out loud. It's a bit stilted. Instead, say something like, "I notice and act on every opportunity that presents itself." It's very important to take any affirmation you read and modify it to suit your own way of speaking so that you are speaking naturally to yourself, not just reading what someone else wrote for you. Be natural and be easy!

- Stick to one or two themes at a time. You don't want to muddy the waters by saying affirmations for every single change you want to make all at once. Let one or two new ideas sink in, and then use their power to help develop subsequent ideas.

- Be relaxed and in a positive frame of mind when you say your affirmations. You want to infuse them with as much positive emotion as possible — think about how awesome you will feel as your dream becomes a reality! Feel that emotion! And smile with your whole being with a 'wow,' look at what you just created! This is where belief comes in place. Always remind yourself that if it exists in your imagination, it already exists for you. It is real. It's not your job to worry about how or when those things will come into your awareness.

- Be persistent, consistent, and do not give up. Don't worry if nothing seems to be happening. You are in the process of automating a thought, and this takes time. Just be happy and positive, and keep repeating your affirmations until the statements feel natural and right to you. This may take anywhere from 30-90 days. Don't do this every now and then. Daily repetition is a must. Once your subconscious accepts the new belief, it will start directing your conscious mind to act in keeping with the new belief.

Use the following positive affirmations as inspiration. Use them as they are, or modify them to suit your individual needs:

- Today I feel great. I feel wonderful!
- I am attracting that which is in harmony with my intention
- I am clear about what I want
- I am blessed
- I recognize that I am the creator in all areas of my life
- I am capable to do anything I set my mind on
- I recognize that I am already succeeding in all facets of my life
- I have all the money that I need to do anything that I want to do or want to possess
- I am financially secure
- I see absolute and continuing abundance
- I have the power to attract abundance whenever I want it
- Money flows to me easily
- I appreciate life
- I choose to do more of what I like
- I listen to my intuition and I trust my inner wisdom
- I see myself in perfect health

- I see myself in absolute prosperity
- I am supported by the limitless Universe in all that I need
- Every day, I am getting better and better in every area of my life
- I am healthy, wealthy, and growing spiritually
- I am attracting all the resources I need to succeed in my life
- I have the courage to act on my inspiration
- I can do whatever I set my sights on
- I have true friends who know me and encourage me
- With God, all things are possible

Feel free to add any affirmations that resonate with you!

Add "I believe that" in front for each statement to see an even better effect.

4. Visualize yourself as already having succeeded in changing those beliefs.

Make a note of how your life will change with the new beliefs. Think of all the benefits you will have by developing new positive beliefs. Also think about the consequences of not changing your old limiting beliefs. This will help motivate you and keep you on track. As you start building new beliefs, it is extremely important that you visualize yourself as having already internalized these beliefs. Start talking in the present tense when you talk or think about these new positive beliefs. Say, "I have healthy eating habits," or "I have money for everything that I need to do or want."

Visualization is a powerful tool and we will return to it in more detail later on in the book.

5. Observe yourself and note every time your actions are not consistent with your beliefs.

Your actions should match your thoughts and words to create and sustain your belief system.

A lack of action indicates lack of conviction in your belief. It shows that you have not internalized it at the subconscious level.

Let's say you'd like to trim down your weight, and you are saying all the right affirmations to internalize this belief, but if you are not working out, then what you're telling your subconscious is that you don't want to lose weight, which then strengthens your negative beliefs around weight loss. No action towards your newly-formed positive beliefs will have an adverse affect on the outcome.

Your actions are your thermometer, which tells you whether you are strengthening positive beliefs or negative beliefs. Your actions speak volumes on what you truly believe.

Nothing is possible without efforts. In the same kind of work where a man becomes very successful, there are other people who struggle to do the same thing. The same opportunity opens the door to the unlimited possibilities for someone, whereas others struggle to find a success. If someone achieved the success, that means it has possibilities. You can also do that. You need to follow your beliefs. You have to make continuous efforts.

It requires effort, perseverance, and patience to follow your beliefs. That is why you need to internalize them. Once your subconscious accepts the new beliefs, it will start directing your conscious mind to act in keeping with the new belief.

6. Suspend your disbelief.

Suspension of disbelief is when you are willing to suspend your own critical capabilities and believe the unbelievable. In order for your new belief to reach the subconscious level, you have to consciously learn to suspend your disbelief in whatever new belief you're trying to form.

In the world of fiction, you are often required to believe in a story that you would never accept in the real world. In order to enjoy such movies, the audience engages in a phenomenon known as 'suspension of disbelief', in which you are making a conscious decision to set aside your disbelief and learn to ignore the fact that it isn't real.

You will always act, react, and interact in ways that are believable. Therefore, the new belief that you are trying to establish may be in conflict with what you believe currently. That is why, with consistent effort, you must ignore your disbeliefs as you try to internalize the new belief.

The concept of suspending one's disbelief is no different than hypnotism. Subjects in a hypnotic trance are allowing the hypnotist to access their subconscious mind without any effort by knowingly stopping any conscious thinking.

But how can we do the same without employing drastic measures like hypnotism? Well, these same results can be achieved through meditation. To give you a brief understanding, when we meditate, we are essentially quieting our thinking mind and allowing direct access to our subconscious, where anything is possible. Meditation will be discussed in further detail later in the book.

When utilizing your self-talk, the tendency is to continuously check the results, and in the process you create a disbelief in your speaking which registers as bad feelings that will strengthen your old belief even more. As soon as you notice that your feelings are not in accordance with what you are speaking, learn to suspend the disbelief in your spoken words. Until you have internalized your new beliefs at the subconscious level, be consistent in your effort of changing them. Have patience as you practice this, and with time, your new belief will become as true as fact.

7. Do not feel guilty. Instead be grateful for the progress.

Have a definite plan of action to correct negative beliefs. Every time you notice that you are falling back, repeat the new belief three times in your mind to counter thoughts of any negative beliefs. Do not blame yourself or feel guilty for your present condition. Sometimes people feel sorry for themselves, thinking they should not have done this or said that. Asking yourself how you could have allowed yourself to put on that extra weight or let an important relationship drift away is not going to help.

Recognize that your old negative beliefs caused it, but let your new positive beliefs take care of the problems. Dwelling in the past, looking for reasons and things to blame is not the way to bring about positive changes. Look ahead, visualize positive results and stay with your positive beliefs. This is the only way you can start seeing the changes you want in your life. Believe your circumstances have changed and act accordingly.

Be grateful each and every day for the progress you have made, small or large. Remember, as I said earlier, gratitude is a great multiplier. Have fun and enjoy the process.

Plant what you want to reap.

If you want rice, you need to plant rice, not wheat.

Your belief system should be similarly consistent with what you want. Negative beliefs are like weeds that destroy the good crops. If you want to reap a good harvest, in addition to planting the right seeds and nurturing them, you also need to take out the weeds. Our negative thoughts are the weeds that you need to yank out.

Unfortunately, negativity is all around us and is all too easy to attract.

Positive beliefs are like good habits. A good habit is formed when you consistently repeat an activity over a period of time. Affirmations need to be repeated in the same manner to develop positive beliefs.

IN A NUTSHELL

- *To be successful in life and to achieve your dreams, it is extremely important to replace your negative beliefs with positive ones.*
- *It is not until you change your belief system that your dreams begin to come alive.*
- *Find and replace the old limiting beliefs within you. This requires lots of effort but it is worth it at the end.*
- *Accept that change is required. The only thing which is constant in our life is change. Change is inevitable to change our life for the better.*
- *Your actions must align with your thoughts and words to create and sustain your belief system.*

SECTION II

LAW OF EXPECTATION

Chapter 7
YOUR EXPECTATIONS SHAPE YOUR REALITY

> *"Achievement is largely the product of steadily raising one's level of aspiration and expectation."*
> — *Jack Nicklaus*

There have been scientific studies done on how expectation can affect an outcome and influence behavior.

In a landmark study of school teachers and students in a school in California in 1968, Robert Rosenthal and Lenore Jacobson started their study by conducting an IQ test. Then, ignoring the results of the IQ tests, they randomly selected a group of students and told the teachers that these particular students were expected to do better than the others based on the results of their IQ test. The teachers in turn communicated these expectations to the students. At the end of the academic year, the researchers conducted another IQ test, which showed that the students who were told they were expected to do well indeed did better than others. Their expectations had translated into reality.

Our expectations can affect reality and can create self-fulfilling prophecies as a result. As parents, we create expectations in our children, which act as either enablers or limitations for them. In the absence of an external stimulus, like the researchers creating the expectation in the above study, our beliefs trigger our expectations.

If you believe you are happy, loved, and at peace, you will start expecting it. That expectation can create a self-fulfilling prophecy.

Many times people's pain decreases as soon as the doctor's name is heard. In some places they create a belief that they will be cured. Therefore, sometimes simple medicines show an exceptional effect.

That is the basis of all healing: the expectation that a healing mode — whatever that mode is — will work. Even if you believe that your body will spontaneously heal on its own without any assistance, you are creating the expectation that your body has miraculous healing capabilities (which it does).

But if a patient believes and expects that nothing will work, then all the drugs, surgical procedures, and treatment protocols in the world can do absolutely nothing because the mind will reject it.

The mind is constantly jumping to conclusions about the world we live in and who we are. We experience reality through our sense organs and conscious mind. Based on that, we create our beliefs and thereafter form our expectations about how things will be in the future. The expectations we form are based on the beliefs we hold as well as personal experiences.

For example, you will probably expect to fail if you have been telling yourself all your life that you aren't good at anything. Or you may expect to succeed if you believe that you are clever and resourceful enough to overcome obstacles. You may expect to be rejected when you ask someone out if you have had this experience before, or if you feel that you are unworthy of this person's attention.

The thing is, these expectations tend to become self-fulfilling prophecies if they are given enough mental, emotional, and physical energy on your part. If you expect to fail, you will. If you expect to succeed, you will. If you expect to look ridiculous while dancing, you will probably misstep quite often and end up looking silly. If you expect to get rejected when you ask someone out, you may unwittingly say exactly the wrong thing, guaranteeing that rejection. What you think about comes about. It's really that simple. You take action based on your beliefs and expectations. This is automatic!

The thing to remember is that negative expectations are based on negative beliefs. It is an automatic and self-fulfilling process and you will revert to behavior that will prove your expectation. The instant you prove your expectation/ belief to yourself, you reinforce and strengthen it. This is why changing your beliefs is essential for changing your expectation, your actions, and your results!

Let's say you're a competitive athlete. You believe that you perform poorly under pressure. Your pre-game rituals are all about stress relief and getting into the 'zone.' Here are two scenarios you can use to transform this belief into one that serves you:

- You can create a belief that pre-event nervousness actually improves your performance by elevating the levels of hormones like adrenaline. Therefore, you expect that the increase in heart rate, perspiration, and the like are positive signs that you are primed and ready for action! There is no reason to choke under pressure, because the pressure is enhancing your performance.

- You can create a belief that pressure makes you mentally and physically sharper. Therefore, you will expect that your mind and body will work together perfectly in competition. You expect that you won't second-guess yourself, your movements will be synchronized, you will anticipate your opponents' moves, and more.

If you work on creating these beliefs, you will develop an expectation that pressure actually helps you. You will find that you will perform exceptionally well when the pressure is on, and, ironically, you will probably fall well short of your personal best efforts when you know there is no pressure (such as when you are the clear favorite). At that point, you will want to find out what your beliefs and expectations are when the competition isn't much of a challenge!

You can use that scenario in any area of your life: social engagements, relationships, career, health, spirituality — anything. What are some of your current expectations in the following areas of your life? Here are a few examples:

- *Health: I expect to be healthy when I eat right and exercise.*
- *Wealth: I expect that it's easy to make money.*
- *Career/purpose: I am good at what I do and I will rise to the top of my profession.*
- *Relationships: I am good at building lasting relationships.*
- *Spirituality: I have a strong sense of oneness with all there is.*

It's important to identify your expectations and write them down, which will compel you to take action and get positive results.

Once you believe something is possible, and you start expecting it to materialize, keep that momentum going! Reinforce the belief and expectation with the language you use, the actions you take, and visualization.

Inspired Action

Letting go and allowing is not something many of us are comfortable with. But letting go doesn't mean sitting idly by. It means being okay with the process and letting it unfold, even if you think things aren't going exactly as you had planned. It means you take inspired action and resist the urge to doubt your intuitive guidance.

Let your Higher Self (or the supreme energy) take the control. You have put out there what you want. Believe in it, take inspired action, and surrender. Just like when you order a meal at a restaurant, you expect it to arrive. You don't go into the kitchen every five minutes and bother the chef. You let the food come to you when it's ready!

Be open to receiving inner guidance and allow yourself to take action on it! You can never know it all. There are always elements of any situation you could not have anticipated, known about, or controlled, and there is nothing wrong or shameful in asking for guidance. Who could be better to ask for guidance than your Higher Self, rather than some other person whose agenda may not be aligned with yours?

Many people pray, but then they forget to listen to their inner voice, which provides the answer to their prayer. This is why often we believe that our prayers go unanswered. Even if you don't pray, you have surely had flashes of intuition, moments of inspiration, and a certain 'knowing' about things, people, or events. Did you listen to this wisdom? Did you act on it? Ask yourself, why is it easier to follow the guidance of other people than your own Higher Self? Let your intuition, feelings, dreams or hunches guide you.

The answers are always given, but you have to be open to receiving them and you have to allow yourself to take inspired action. Don't sit around and wait for guidance. Simply go about your life with heightened awareness. Do what you feel is right and good for you, don't second-guess it, don't rationalize to yourself why it can't work, and don't disbelieve it just because it is not how others do things.

When you feel good, you know you are moving in the right direction. When you feel stressed, upset, angry, jealous, fearful, or anxious, you know you are moving in the wrong one.

Why is this a big deal? We humans are very good at talking ourselves into anything. It's easy to get sucked into logic and reason when in your gut, you know it's wrong for you. Don't compromise. Allow yourself to be guided and allow the process to unfold as you take inspired action.

IN A NUTSHELL

- *The expectations we form are based on the beliefs we hold, as well as our personal experiences.*
- *Our expectancies can affect reality and create self-fulfilling prophecies as a result.*
- *Changing your beliefs is essential for changing your expectation, your actions, and your results.*
- *The thing to remember is that negative expectations are based on negative beliefs.*
- *It is an automatic and self-fulfilling process and you will revert to behavior that will prove your expectations.*

Chapter 8
EXPECT AND RECEIVE

"Expectations create and shape reality."
— *Debasish Mridha*

At every stage of life, we need to take a closer look at how our life is in the present and evaluate it by asking ourselves some questions:

"Am I where I want to be?" "Am I happy with my career?"

"Have I earned enough money?" "Have I cultivated good relationships?" "Am I healthy?"

Answers to these questions may bring forth deep introspection. You will better understand the contribution you have made towards your life that has brought you to where you are today, and realize that, knowingly or unknowingly, your expectations manifested your current reality. This is how the law of expectation works.

List all that has not turned out as you wished and convert those to positive expectations. Once you make a shift from negative to positive in the way you expect things, the law of expectation will show its magic.

Expectations are influenced by our beliefs and the conditioning of our mind. When you continuously think about your positive expectations and are sure you will receive that which you desire, it will make your beliefs stronger. Hence to manifest your expectations, it is important to examine your beliefs.

Suppose you desire to increase your income. Your intention is conveyed to the Universe. But if in your mind you believe it cannot be done, then you will start expecting that it is difficult to get what you want and ultimately you will not have what you asked for. Whereas for the Universe, there is no difference between giving you a hundred dollars or a million.

Here are some useful tips to make the law of expectation work for you.

Avoid the negative chatter: Your mind can be your best friend or worst enemy, so what you feed it is very important. Avoid negative talk, complaining, arguing, being fearful, or feeling powerless. Separate yourself from people who sap your energy and leave you feeling miserable or not confident. Detach yourself from the negative and instead read inspirational books and articles. Associate with positive people. More importantly, watch your internal dialogue and be kind with the words you use for yourself. Think of how you would speak of those you care for or respect. Learn to talk and think about yourself in the same manner.

Always expect the best: Whatever you focus on grows. Start to train your mind to think only good thoughts by developing a strong focus and thinking about things that make you happy. Don't give your attention to anything unwanted. Be the watchman at the gate of your mind. If you catch yourself thinking an unwanted thought, simply shake your head and let the thought dissipate. Say positive affirmations such as, "I deserve and expect the best," or "I always attract all that is good into my life." These are very powerful. By repeating such affirmations, you start expecting the best for yourself.

Believe and have faith: You believe that your desire will be manifested and you expect it to happen, but sometimes, while sailing through rough waters in the sea of life, you may encounter doubts and uncertainties. For example, let us say that you desire money. You believe and expect to get it. You begin to do very well in your business, money is flowing in, and you are very happy.

Suddenly, your business starts slowing down or you hit a setback, and you become worried and start doubting your beliefs. Perhaps you start thinking, "What if I lose everything I have worked for?" If this negative expectation is entertained for too long, you will lose all that you have built towards. When this happens, have faith that things will work out, and block all negative thoughts from influencing the positive beliefs and expectations that you have cultivated. Have faith that something good will come out of your situation. Believe in it, and have the right expectations. Challenges are only temporary and are sometimes sent to test your belief. Continue to practice your faith and what you desire will certainly come to fruition.

Eliminate worries from your life: If you've ever observed a small child, you would notice that he or she has faith, is happy without reason and is always ready to experiment and learn. Worry, anxiety, and other negative emotions are a foreign concept for them. As a child, you too were carefree and unaffected by your surroundings.

Then what happens as we grow up? Our mind gets conditioned by society, people, and circumstances around us and we slowly start to focus on the lack in our lives instead of the abundance that exists. Worrying is something that we learn to do as adults which only attracts more of what we don't want in our lives. Before we take on a new opportunity, we may start thinking about the negatives or the possible problems we may encounter.

Don't get me wrong here. It is very important to look at both sides of the coin. But when we focus too much on the negative side, it prevents us from taking any steps forward.

This is why it's very important to eliminate any and all worries, which only limit you from your true potential. Worrying serves no purpose. Instead, choose to live in the moment, exactly the way that a child would. Then, why would you need to waste your time thinking about the worries? Live in the moment and free your mind.

Be clear about what you want: I once met an old gentleman who seemed to be displeased with the way his life had turned out. "I wanted to do so much in life, but couldn't do much. My life is a waste." He was dejected.

I asked him, "What is it that you expected from your life?" He thought for a while but had no concrete answer. Most often we give too much attention to "could not do enough" without even evaluating what it is that we truly want.

I have heard people saying, "I want a good life." But what is your definition of a good life? It is a very subjective term and the definition differs from person to person. It is very important to be clear and specific about what you want — only then will the Universe be able to give it to you.

Take action: Suppose you wish to go on a vacation and expect and imagine it to be a certain way. It will not manifest unless you take action. You need to plan your itinerary, book your tickets, pack your bags, and board the flight. If you just sit at home and expect to have a fabulous holiday, it will not happen. Take action. Without action, your dreams will only remain a dream. Action is the key element in all of this and whatever positive expectations you practice will be fruitless without taking the appropriate action.

Learn to receive: I knew of a girl who was always unhappy and put herself in the victim zone. She would always complain, "I never really get what I want." She didn't realize that she had become accustomed to saying 'no' to what she got. If her friends bought her a present, she would say, "No, no, I am fine. I don't really need it," though she would actually want it. The result was that eventually everyone stopped getting her presents.

To benefit from the law of expectation, you need to be a good receiver. Receiving is also an art. You need to be grateful for what you have received. I have met some people who are fabulous receivers. They accept any gift given to them with so much humility and grace that the person giving the gift feels so important and happy.

Here's a small exercise that will help you harness the energy of the law of expectation.

- Write down your desires on a sheet of paper.
- Write down beside each desire whether you believe or doubt that these will manifest.
- Now one by one, evaluate your doubts versus the desires and identify the limiting beliefs or the negative statements that come forth.
- Transform these negative statements to powerful positive ones.
- Say to yourself, "I willingly release all the fears and doubts associated with my desire (you can write down the desire)."
- Then say, "I willingly receive (your desire) right here and right now."

Practice this until it becomes a new self-affirming belief. Feel how amazing it will be when you are living your dreams. Always end with love and thankfulness for that which will be.

IN A NUTSHELL

- *Expectations are influenced by our beliefs and the conditioning of our minds.*

- *Whatever you focus on grows. Start to train your mind to think only good thoughts by developing a strong focus and thinking about things that make you happy.*

- *Challenges are only temporary and are sometimes sent to test your belief. Continue to practice your faith and what you desire will certainly come to fruition.*

- *It is very important to be clear and specific about what you want. Only then will the Universe be able to give it to you.*

- *Taking action is very critical for your success. Whatever positive expectations you practice will be fruitless without taking appropriate action.*

Chapter 9
POWER OF EXPECTATION

"Don't lower your expectations to meet your performance. Raise your level of performance to meet your expectations. Expect the best of yourself, and then do what is necessary to make it a reality."

— Ralph Marston

Immediately after graduating from pharmacy school I started work in a town called Valsad at a pharmaceutical company. I had a lot of free time on my hands and I developed a keen interest in palmistry and astrology and I took some lessons. As practice, I started reading the palms of people around me, like those of my uncle, aunt, and neighbors. I was no master but had learned enough to tell someone a few facts about their past. I would correctly guess their past, which gave them confidence and belief in my abilities.

However, this led them to assume I could also predict the future. One of our neighbors wanted his daughter to get married and brought her over so that I could read her palm. They asked me, "When will she get married?" I obviously had no idea but gave them an answer anyway. Because they believed in my prediction so strongly, she did in fact get married exactly when I had predicted. They didn't know I had made it up, but their belief in my word was so strong that it became a reality. My popularity increased thereafter.

By then my sister Asha was married and living in an adjacent town named Bardoli, which was about 88 km from Valsad. I would visit her during the weekends. She came to know about my palm-reading skills and told her friends about it. Whenever I would visit, her friends would flock around me with great expectations of me to tell them about their future. Slowly, word spread and people began saying that my predictions about their future were accurate.

Everyone was curious about their own future. By reading their hands, I would first tell them about their past, which was useful in validating the facts about that person. They started believing in me and in my forecast about their future. The questions would be like, "When will my daughter get married?" or "When will I get a job?" I would just look at their hands and say whatever date came to mind, and to my surprise, these readings transformed into reality.

Now, when I look back, I can very well relate this to the law of expectation. When I gave a certain prediction, people believed it because of their belief in me and consequently started expecting the result. This combination worked its magic.

Simply put, the law of expectation basically says that whatever one presumes, with emotion and belief, becomes a self-fulfilling prophecy. Hence, according to this law, whenever you expect the best, it will happen, and whenever you expect the worst, that will happen, too.

Sometimes we have strong expectations regarding the negative things that occur in our lives. We often say, "I knew that was not going to work," or "This was bound to happen one day." When we think about any of the above statements we are creating that belief and feeding it to our subconscious mind.

A friend of mine, let's call her Julie, was working as a personal assistant to the CEO of a company. Julie was doing extremely well at work and was often praised by her colleagues. However, one day her sister began teasing her and accused Julie of having a careless attitude which she said may one day cost Julie her job.

Day by day, the negative comments began taking root in her mind, which started affecting her performance at work. Though she was intelligent and good at what she did, she began making some serious mistakes. Julie's efforts to improve made no difference and her performance at work continued to suffer. As fate would have it, Julie lost her job due to neglectful behavior. That day, in so many words, her sister said to her, "I told you so." The negative expectations her sister had about her influenced her beliefs greatly, which she internalized and began expecting that one day she might lose her job.

It is of utmost importance that you feed your subconscious mind with expectations that are in line with your beliefs. Whatever you anticipate with earnest desire will manifest. Did you know that right now, your life and body are a result of your prior conscious and subconscious expectations? Did you know that because of the law of expectation, what you expect as 'good' or 'bad' will, in fact, be drawn to you, whether you like it or not?

If your habitual thoughts reflect self-doubt and limiting beliefs, then you will surely have reasons to complain. Just as you expect the best and receive the best, when you expect things to be difficult and when you focus on lack and hardship, you will attract more of what you do not want into your life.

Your expectations are brought about by your self-image and beliefs. Your beliefs are the foundation of your thoughts and feelings; it's why you think the way you do and why you take the actions you take — it is all based on your belief system and what you expect in your life.

Is it possible to shift from negative to positive expectations? Yes, certainly!

What you really need to do is, as they say, to knock the 'T' off the 'can't.' Change your thinking from negative to positive. By doing so, you will shift from having self-doubt to having powerful expectations. Faithfully focus on what you truly want and believe that it will come to pass and you can achieve anything you set your mind to. Every time you notice that your expectations are not in line with what you want, make a conscious effort to change it. What is an expectation? It is what we assume will happen in the future, which has not happened yet.

We often have beliefs, such as, "This is too difficult for me," or "I don't think I will be able to do it." Even though you want the best that life has to offer you, your desire is dying its own death in the conscious mind, and the assailant is your own negative expectations. All you need to do is change your thinking to "This is easy for me," or "I can do anything I want to," or "I deserve the best." Expectations, both positive and negative, are nothing but our assumptions about future outcomes. Why not choose positive?

You can blast through the limiting ceiling in your mind by being positive and establishing powerful, self-supporting beliefs. By doing so, your faith will increase and your expectations will shift to that of 'expecting to receive' rather than 'expecting to fail.' Before you know it, you will see the rewards from your efforts.

Rather than giving your attention to what you do not want, focus on what you do want. Visualize your dreams as if you were already living them. Your thoughts will impress upon your body as to what to do, which ignites action. Your actions are a result of your beliefs and expectations. Positive expectations will yield positive action.

Likewise, negative expectations will bring on action that you may realize later as being unwanted and that will make you ask yourself, "Why did I do that?" That is why it is imperative to think positively with the expectation to receive the desired outcome.

The more proactive you are in attaining your desires, the more you will set positive energy into motion, which will attract a positive outcome.

Many times when you desire something and start expecting it, it may take some time to materialize. You may start with a strong positive belief, and as time passes, you might start to run out of patience. Then your self-doubts slowly start creeping in. As time passes, your expectations about the result slowly make a shift from positive to negative. And finally whatever you desired does not materialize in your life and you feel all this is useless and that you are not destined for a good life.

To avoid such pitfalls, patience is extremely important when you are following the law of expectation. When you go to a restaurant and order a few dishes, each dish takes its own time to come. Here, you don't lose your patience as you know that it will surely come. Similarly, when you ask something of the Universe, you need to be sure that you will be receiving it. If you ask for a hundred dollars, you might receive it the very next day. But if you ask for a million dollars, you need to give some time to the Universe to manifest the same.

Recently, I went to a Mont Blanc store with the intention to buy a black messenger bag. I had wanted this bag for a long time and had a strong desire to get it. When I went to the store, the storekeeper told me that it was not available in black, but I could get the brown one instead. I refused, because I was very clear that I wanted a black bag. He said he could order the black one and I could get it the following week.

Well, I never found the time to go back to the store and forgot about the bag altogether. A few days later, our friends Raju and Nisha were visiting us from California. They brought with them gifts for Mina and me. When I opened the present, to my surprise, I was amazed to see the same Mont Blanc black messenger bag that I had desired. I expected to own it and my desire was so strong that it was bound to show up in my life, and in this case, in the most unexpected way. This is how the law of expectation works.

The law of expectation tells us that whatever one expects becomes, with confidence, a self-fulfilling prophecy. And this applies to the good as well as the bad things in life.

Life is simple and beautiful. We just need to align ourselves with its flow. Our job is to expect and allow it to happen in its own timing.

IN A NUTSHELL

- *Expectation is what we assume will happen in the future which has not happened yet.*

- *The law of expectation basically says that whatever one presumes, along with emotion and belief, becomes a self-fulfilling prophecy.*

- *If you allow it, the expectations of people around you can easily modify your behavior for better, or for worse.*

- *Changing your beliefs from negative to positive can shift your self-doubts to powerful expectation.*

- *As per the law of expectation, whatever one expects becomes, with confidence, a reality. And this applies to the good as well as the bad things in life.*

SECTION III

LAW OF IMAGINATION

Chapter 10
WRITE THE SCRIPT OF YOUR LIFE

"Anyone who lives within their means suffers from a lack of imagination."
— *Oscar Wilde*

Everything that appeared in reality, every great achievement, every big attainment, first came to mind as thought and then converted into a reality. Imagination is part of our nature. We cannot live without visualizing something. While sitting in one place, we go somewhere else. We see the unseen places. We feel them from insight. Visualization takes our thinking forward. Deep thinking increases the power of imagination.

All of us engage in the process of imagination or visualization, knowingly or unknowingly. For example, let's say you're taking a trip to see the Niagara Falls. Before you actually go, you visualize the whole trip: driving into the park, walking up to the falls, taking the boat ride on the river bringing you closer to the falls, having your pictures taken, and so on. The entire process is imagined as soon as a decision is made. And it happens exactly the way you had imagined.

The flip side of that is the negative visualization we do daily without even realizing it. Let's say your son is out and normally comes home at an expected time, but somehow on this day an hour or two have passed and he still hasn't come home, and you haven't even heard from him. Now you start worrying and begin to imagine every possible negative outcome, maybe even proving you right.

Unfortunately, this sort of visualization is more routine then we'd like, which stems from our fears, doubts, and worries. Instead, the purpose is to utilize the power of your imagination only towards what is positive and wanted in your life; because when you visualize a particular outcome, with the right emotions attached to it, you are setting it into motion.

Imagination isn't just idle daydreaming. There is nothing wrong with daydreaming, because at that moment your mind is relaxed, open, and even playful. Daydreaming can be vague; as our mind continuously hops from one thought to another, whereas our imagination can be directed.

You can create all sorts of fanciful and even improbable solutions to any problem through imagination. Sometimes, one of those solutions might actually work, or spark other solutions!

It all starts with a thought. When we imagine, we create powerful images in our mind around that thought. If there is worry, anxiety, or any negative emotion attached to that thought, we are creating mental images of what might go wrong.

A friend of mine was once involved in a bad car accident. After the accident, when we spoke, I realized that he may have absorbed this image from the television or the news. It replayed in his mind a number of times and every time, subconsciously, he would render it with additional details. One day, while he was driving on the highway, he was hit by another car and, not surprisingly, the accident happened in the exact same way that he had visualized it. When the same thoughts keep on repeating in our mind, they gain power and manifest physically. Our mind is incredibly powerful, and so is our imagination. So when you direct your imagination, you need to train yourself to imagine only the positive outcome.

Successful people from all fields use creative thinking and visualization as a tool to achieve what they are looking for in life.

Albert Einstein asked questions and looked at things in ways that no one else did. He believed in possibility thinking, meaning exploring what is creatively possible, usually way beyond the boundaries of what you know. You need to keep pushing the envelope, testing, and probing to break through the boundaries of the tried and familiar. This not only gives you the permission to do extraordinary things but also gives you the opportunity to do so.

Einstein used visualization at the age of 16 when he discovered that the speed of light was always constant. He believed that visual understanding was the most important form of education and was more important than knowledge.

Einstein later wrote, "I am enough of an artist to draw freely upon my imagination. Imagination is more important than knowledge. Knowledge is limited. Imagination circles the world."

The law of imagination lets you write your life's story the way you want and lets you rewrite any part of it you are not satisfied with through creative visualization.

Creative visualization is an elementary technique for creating situations of your choice in your life. It is the process in which you use your thought power to consciously create imagery of the things or situations you want to attract in your life. Mastering creative visualization grants you direct control over your thoughts at the subconscious level and enables you to harness the creative power of your thoughts to create the life of your dreams.

The better you visualize the future you want, the better your chances to make it happen. A person can visualize the complete process in the mind. The mind can analyze the possibilities and create a mental picture. Great people in every field know what they are going to create. They know every single detail about their idea and they know it's going to be possible. They have a clear vision in visualization. Creative visualization uses the power of the mind and is the power behind every success. Whatever the mind can imagine and trust, it can accomplish.

It starts with a clear vision — a vision so clear and precise that you are willing to do whatever it takes to make it a reality.

If you ever find yourself complaining of the things that are not happening right in your life, or you are not getting what you desire, it is time to halt and take a stock of your thoughts. Thoughts become very powerful when they are fueled with emotions. Whatever thoughts you focus on will grow. When these thoughts are projected on your mind's eye they become imagery. The conversion of these images into reality depends on the kind of emotions these thoughts are fed with. You have a choice to feed them with either doubt, worry, and anxiety; or with happiness, love, and gratitude.

Most people have no control over their thoughts, and think negatively most of the time. This brings negative results into their lives. It is when you become conscious of this mighty power of creative imagination, study it and learn how to use it effectively, that positive results start arriving. You can change almost anything in your life through law of imagination.

Our creative visualization process often gets influenced by our old beliefs. Say that you want to score the highest grade in your exams. However, in the past, you did study hard but did not succeed. Somewhere in your subconscious, a belief was born that even if you studied hard, you wouldn't get desirable grades.

You come to know about creative visualization and want to try it out. Now when you are visualizing your goal, the belief that is growing in your subconscious peeps out. Suddenly, a self-doubt creeps in. The final result is you are not successful despite the visualization. Any negative belief cripples the creative visualization process. So, how do you get rid of this? By working on your beliefs first. By recognizing, acknowledging, and transforming the negative beliefs into positive ones.

The law of imagination can work wonders with our health. Creative visualization can be used in creating and maintaining good health. Our physical, mental, and emotional states are closely linked. There is constant communication between the three.

Any disease is first conceived in the thought. When our mind conceives disease or sickness, it conveys the same message to the body and the body reacts accordingly. This phenomenon can be reversed by imagination through the mind. Hence, the disease, if it has not affected the physical body past the point of no return, can be uprooted from the mind itself. In other words, as soon as you detect the first sign of sickness, utilize your imagination to heal yourself before you even need to. By visualizing every day that you are healthy, you are sending a powerful signal to your body and thus illnesses can be avoided.

Never hold back when you creatively visualize. Never censor your imagination with 'reality' or what you think can or can't be accomplished or had. Many years ago, people were convinced that the Earth was flat, and they insisted that whoever sailed to the Earth's end would fall off the edge, never to be seen again. This notion was based on people's observation of the world — nobody had ever been high enough on dry land to see the curvature of the earth, and so they didn't believe that the Earth wasn't flat at all. Imagine what you want, regardless of what reality looks like. You can create a new reality.

Your thoughts are endowed with a creative power that molds your life, and you attract what you think about. You can visualize different circumstances and situations, and thus create a life of your aspirations. By changing your thoughts and mental images, you change your life. You can be the author of the book that is your life.

IN A NUTSHELL

- *When you visualize a particular outcome, with the right emotions attached to it, you are setting it into motion.*

- *Visualization is essential to send your dreams to your subconscious mind for the planning of steps you need to take to make it a reality.*

- *Successful people from all fields use creative thinking and visualization as a tool to achieve what they are looking for in life.*

- *Be watchful of your old negative beliefs because they do influence your creative visualization process.*

- *Imagination can work wonders in creating the life of your choice more than solely hard work.*

Chapter 11
THE ART OF VISUALIZING

"Everyone visualizes whether he knows it or not.
Visualizing is the great secret of success"
— **Geneviève Berhre**

During my speaking tours, when I talk about visualizing my goals, some people ask, "Will creative visualization work for me?"

But let me tell you that creative visualization, just like any other natural law, works for everyone. What you need to remember is that you are continuously visualizing and creating what you see in your physical world through your thoughts. It is an unfailing law.

Imagining can be described as the process of creating a mental image or intention of what you want to happen or feel.

For instance, let's say you're in search of a spouse. First, you need to know the type of person you're looking for and the qualities they should possess. Once you have these details, the next step is to create an image of the person of your dreams with vivid details. You should imagine feeling happy and loved in their presence and you should note the exact emotions you would like to experience when you are with them, all in your imagination.

If you continue to visualize every day with the same feelings, you will, without any doubt, attract the right life partner in no time.

The knack of visualization lies in imagining the end state. Think about what it would be like to have achieved the success you want. What would it feel like to be in your dream home? What would it be like to have a million dollars in your bank account? What would it feel like to be at the pinnacle of success in your career?

How does it work? Outcomes in the physical world are first created in the mental world. Let us go a little deeper and look at our mind. Our mind has two levels – the conscious and the subconscious. The conscious mind is the analytical or logical mind. It is our waking state through which we operate on a daily basis. We make choices and think of ideas, set goals, and daydream through our conscious mind. The conscious mind communicates with the outside world and the inner self through speech, pictures, writing, physical movement, and thoughts.

The subconscious mind, on the other hand, is the storehouse of all memories and past experiences, those that have been repressed through trauma and those that have simply been consciously forgotten and are no longer important to us. It's from these memories and experiences that our beliefs, habits, and behaviors are influenced.

As I had said earlier, our mind can be compared to a computer. The keyboard and the screen is the conscious mind, whereas all that goes behind it, all that runs the show — the CPU — is the subconscious mind. Through the conscious mind we think and plan and set goals. We visualize the things we want to attract in our life. It is like entering data and seeing results.

The key is to leave the 'how' to the subconscious.

Once you have created dreams and goals with your conscious mind, you need to communicate it to your subconscious. If you let your conscious mind take over, there is a greater chance of your goals not materializing. The problem with this approach is that as soon as you start planning consciously, it sows the seeds of doubt in your mind. When the conscious mind is planning, it will look at all the limitations. On the other hand, the subconscious mind has unlimited potential and it can make things happen in miraculous ways, even if they seem logically impossible or improbable.

For example, let's say that you are currently making $50,000 annually and instead want to make $250,000 a year. The moment you start planning it consciously, it would seem improbable. You will start thinking in terms of your current job and skills and how you could make it happen with what you have got. But the fact that you are making $50,000 a year means your current resources are unlikely to get you to $250,000. If you plan it consciously, doubts will soon arise, saying, "I am not sure if it is possible." Your old beliefs will attack with full force.

This is where the art of visualization will help. Start visualizing the changes in the lifestyle you can have with $250,000 a year. Add as many details as possible. What kind of house would you live in? What car will you drive? Where would you travel? What kind of wardrobe would you have? What amazing presents would you buy your loved ones? And so on. Once you start visualizing with good, joyful feelings you will be able to send your desire — to make $250,000 a year — to your subconscious mind, which will start working on a plan. Your subconscious mind is free of all limitations. If you let it do its job and listen to it, it will soon give you directions in terms of ideas, thoughts, hunches, or instincts. All of a sudden, you may want to call somebody or do something that will lead you there.

When you are consciously visualizing a particular result or solution, remember that it is extremely important to visualize in a way that allows you to feel what it is like to already have what you desire. You need to shift your focus to the end result of what you aim to achieve. Creative visualization should be done with a solution in mind, not the problem. If you visualize a problem in your mind, you are giving it more energy to grow.

For example, let's say that you own a business and are currently operating out of a garage. It is inconvenient, and you aim to move to a larger office with more space. You start visualizing, say, a 1000 square foot office space, with vivid details such as the color of the walls, the kind of wood used for the floors, how many glass windows there are, and how the desks are arranged.

As you imagine this, you also feel very happy that you have moved to your dream office. It is very important not to focus on the absence of it in your life. If you focus on the fact that it is very uncomfortable in your garage and that you need to move out fast, the feeling of lack will create a resistance in the manifestation of the end result.

Sometimes you may find it difficult to imagine something that does not exist. As a practice, close your eyes and start to visualize something that you already know and are familiar with. For example, if you have a loving and supportive family, start picturing happy moments you have had with them. Once you develop this habit, imagining the nonexistent will become easy.

Some people may find it difficult to feel the joy that comes from imagining what they want. This is mainly due to preconditioned thoughts that create doubts in our mind. Start visualizing that which is known to you and it will generate joyful feelings, as in the above example. Thinking about your family gives you good feelings. Utilize that same principle when thinking about what you desire. Once you are able to internalize joyful feelings, you can begin visualizing the nonexistent and it will start to manifest in your life.

The art of visualization has dramatic effects. It has helped several successful people to achieve great heights; and it can help you as well. The power of imagination is available to all of us. We just need to tap into it. If practiced regularly with all sincerity, your life's goals will be within your reach.

IN A NUTSHELL

- *Remember that you are continuously visualizing and creating what you see in your physical world through your conscious or subconscious thoughts.*

- *Everything in this world is created first in the mind before it shows up in its physical form.*

- *Visualization has many applications in human development. Regardless of what it is – you want to accomplish something, improve your skills, improve your financial situation, improve your health, remove any fear, replace any negative beliefs — visualization can help.*

- *Visualization is not a magic wand that can bring success overnight, but if it is used properly, visualization will bring improvements that you desire in your life.*

Chapter 12
MANIFESTING YOUR DREAMS

"Imagination is the beginning of creation. You imagine what you desire, you will what you imagine and at last you create what you will."
— **George Bernard Shaw**

Every person has the dream to live their life to the fullest. None of us want to lead a mediocre life. But most often, our dreams get buried along with us in the grave. At the end of the journey of life, we feel that "I should have done that," or "I should have listened to my inner voice," or "I should have followed the signals the Universe was trying to give me," and so on. But by the time we realize this, we have already burnt the bridges behind us.

If you are reading this book and if you have any regrets, it is never too late. You are at the right place. You have opened a door to an opportunity to manifest the life of your dreams. The law of imagination allows you to do that. Having visualized your dreams and ideas in the conscious mind, the next step is to communicate those to your subconscious mind. For this, you need to establish a communication channel between the two. Most people struggle with this because of the mental noise created by numerous thoughts hovering in their mind.

Suppose you are driving. One of your friends calls and asks you, "Hey, what's on your mind?" You instantly reply, "Oh, nothing, really." But if you become aware, there are hundreds of thoughts going on in your mind even during that time. They could be about the conversation you had with your boss, or the bills that you need to pay, or perhaps about your children or spouse or politics. Some of these thoughts may be insignificant, but they exist.

According to research, on average, we get around 60,000 thoughts per day. A few are mundane, most of them are limiting, and the remaining few, if any, are positive. Chatter is continuously going on in our mind. Think of two people sitting in a room trying to talk to each other with a speaker blaring out high-decibel music. It would be difficult to communicate, wouldn't it? Only when the music is turned off can proper communication happen.

Our conscious and subconscious minds face a similar challenge because of too many thoughts, dreams, and ideas going around in our heads. These random thoughts and ideas act as the high-decibel music preventing the subconscious and the conscious from connecting properly. One needs to turn off this music first to be able to communicate.

How do you do that?

You can calm down your conscious mind with meditation. Your goal should be to meditate for 15 minutes every day to start with, and once you can successfully keep your mind at rest, increase the time duration gradually, up to perhaps an hour. Find a comfortable place in your home where you will be free of distractions. Switch off your mobile phone or keep it away. Set an alarm to go off after fifteen minutes.

Close your eyes and focus on your breathing. Feel the air entering your nose and then feel yourself exhale. You should not think or feel anything other than the air entering and leaving your body. Initially, your mind will start wandering as you try to meditate. By focusing on your breathing, you train your mind to focus on the present and cut out the noise. If you feel that your mind is again going in some other direction, focus on your breathing again.

In the beginning, you may not be able to focus for more than a couple of minutes before your mind wanders away. Don't panic – it will take some time to master it. Be patient with the process, and eventually you will begin meditating for 15 minutes straight with no interruptions or distractions.

A word of caution: don't expect it to work on the first day. After all, this chatter in our minds has been going on since we could first consciously form a thought. Any habit takes at least a few weeks to change. When you sit for meditation on the first day, within around 30 seconds, your mind will start jumping all over and the music will start again. As soon as you realize the music has started, go back to breathing. Even though you may not be able to meditate for 15 minutes to begin with, you must give it a try. You will eventually get there.

Once you're done meditating and have quieted down your conscious mind, start visualizing exactly the kind of life you want. Close your eyes and start imagining what you want as if you already have it. This is how you send your desires to your subconscious mind so it can begin planning.

Once the subconscious mind has developed a plan, it needs to be communicated back to the conscious mind for action. The subconscious does that through intuitions, gut feelings, hunches, or even dreams.

The German chemist August Kekulé, who discovered the ring structure of benzene, credits his discovery to a dream. He spent many years trying to work out benzene's molecular structure. He claimed that one day, while thinking about the problem; he dozed off to sleep and had a strange dream of a snake eating its own tail, forming a ring. Kekulé claimed that the dream gave him the idea about the ring structure that would famously become benzene.

We dream many dreams at night but most of us rarely remember them after waking up. It is a great loss, because we miss out on valuable information from our subconscious.

To capture my dreams, I tell myself before going to bed that I will remember and understand my dreams. I keep a notepad and pen next to my bed and when I wake up, the first thing that I do is write down the dreams I had in the night. Sometimes, they don't make sense, but many times, they are instructions from the subconscious mind. Answers to many of my questions have come through my dreams.

Once you get the instruction, act on it with your conscious mind. You will start attracting resources that are identified at the conscious level.

Another way to get instructions is through your intuition, which also bridges the gap between the conscious and the subconscious. Intuition is the process that gives us the ability to 'know' without any logical or analytical reasoning. Often, when we get such a feeling, our logic overshadows it. Sometimes, you get a strong feeling that something is not right or you know that you should take certain action. Most times when such feelings arise, we ignore it, analyze it, or completely dismiss it because it seems illogical. Thus it gets lost and loses its energy.

We are born and brought up in a society where a lot of importance is given to rational thinking. We also form our beliefs accordingly. Though it is generally said that you should use your brains while making any important decisions, there are many successful people in this world who used to follow their heart. They showed their guts by following their intuitions. Listening to your intuition and acting upon it may set the wheels rolling and take you to new horizons.

Gut feelings or hunches are a sensation that we get without knowing the actual underlying reasoning. You may have experienced that you get a hunch to do something, or perhaps out of nowhere, you feel like calling someone you have not been in touch with for ages. You may not act upon it due to hesitation, but a gut feeling or hunch is nature's way of guiding you. If you listen, it will open beautiful doors in your life.

You need to understand that you are the co-creator in the process of universal creation. Believe that your dreams will manifest, even when you don't know how. When you access your core creativity, almost anything is possible. Allow yourself to spend time being mindfully aware of why that dream means so much to you. When you let yourself believe that the impossible can be made possible, you empower yourself to discover all the opportunities available to you.

Once you have the right beliefs and expectations and you are visualizing the end state, you will start attracting situations and people into your life that will turn those expectations into reality. This brings us to the fourth and final law: the law of attraction.

IN A NUTSHELL

- *Learning to meditate is the most critical to control the power of thought and to develop more clarity and happiness.*

- *Meditation is an essential key to quiet down your conscious mind in order to establish a communication channel between subconscious and conscious mind.*

- *It takes lots of practice to master the meditation technique, but don't lose your faith. It will work.*

- *You need to understand that you are the co-creator in the process of universal creation. Believe that your dreams will manifest, even when you don't know how.*

- *When you access your core creativity using meditation to help you, almost anything is possible.*

SECTION IV

LAW OF ATTRACTION

Chapter 13
BE A MAGNET IN YOUR LIFE

"The Law of Attraction states that whatever you focus on, think about, read about, and talk about intensely, you're going to attract more of into your life."
— Jack Canfield

Some desires are so strong that they like to keep you engaged. Some people's dreams become their life. They live with each and every piece of their dream. They do not leave it until it is complete. By combining the desires with the power of the mind, a lot of people have made the impossible possible. There are many people in this world who have experienced this miracle. Many people have applied it in their lives repeatedly. This is the power that takes your positive energy to a new level. You put your infinite energy towards getting a desire and you achieve it.

Whatever you give the most energy to is pulled towards you. The concept that works around this is very interesting. Let's say that you want to buy a particular watch. Suddenly you will start seeing that watch everywhere. That watch was there before, but because you decided to buy one, and because you have that image in your mind, you become more aware.

Our mind is bombarded with millions of images and sounds every day. This can become quite overwhelming. To counter this, we have a defense mechanism, which only allows the things into our minds for which we have created a pathway. There is a guard working 24/7 at the entry point to our mind who grants permission only to those things that are worthy of our attention. As a result, when we consciously think of something we want in our life, be it good health, good relationships, more wealth, a new house, or a new car; we attract the situations, thoughts, people, and the resources that are required to make it happen in our life.

This is nothing but the law of attraction.

Whether we are aware of it or not, the law of attraction is at work in our lives. Many times we hear people say things like, "Oh! It's such a miracle, I was looking for this book for so long and one of my friends just gifted it to me!"

What exactly is the law of attraction and how does it work?

The law of attraction is based on the very laws that govern the Universe.

The Earth and all the other planets in the Solar System work on the law of attraction. The Earth rotates on its own axis and it revolves around the Sun, along with the other planets. This is possible only because of the force of attraction between them. Every visible object attracts each other according to Newton's law of universal gravitation.

Newton's law of gravity defines the attractive force between all objects that possess mass. Understanding the law of gravity, one of the fundamental forces of physics, offers profound insight into the way our Universe functions. The amount of gravitational pull that something possesses is proportional to its mass and distance between it and another object. This explains why we are pulled towards the center of the Earth rather than towards the Sun or another person.

This force of attraction also applies to our thoughts. Therefore, whatever you want will come to you based on the mass and distance of your thoughts about it, be it positive or negative. If you are constantly thinking of what you want, you will increase its mass which will start attracting the object of your desire towards you. Initially what you want may be out of sight, but as you continuously increase its mass, the distance will shorten. So it is not outlandish if we say that thoughts and things attract each other.

Those who have attracted success into their lives have used the same law, knowingly or unknowingly. They think thoughts of abundance, and they do not allow any other negative thoughts to take root in their minds. Their predominant thoughts are of success. Whether they are aware of it or not, their predominant thoughts of abundance are what brought abundance to them. This is the law of attraction in action.

Like attracts like, and hence the only way to manifest something in your outer world is to improvise and amend your inner world which includes your inner vibrations, thoughts, and emotions.

The law of attraction is the most misapplied of the natural laws. Many people think that they must intensely desire and focus on what they want and think of nothing else. But just sitting and wishing isn't going to accomplish anything!

Often people sit down and think one day that they will get everything. But that does not happen. You cannot reach the destination by just sitting and thinking. You know your destination and even if it is visible to you, you have to step up to move towards it.

You need to take action for the outcome you desire. If you do not take the first step, how will you reach towards your goal?

For example, a person who doesn't know anything about music but who dreams of becoming a great composer should be ready to study and learn music to achieve his goal. Applying the law of attraction can make achieving a goal easier and faster, but to manifest it in the real world requires taking action.

There is a very precise way to manifest what you want. It begins with the seed of an idea. That part is easy. The harder part is getting your inner gardener, the subconscious mind, to believe that this seed can grow. Without belief, the gardener will do nothing, saying, "This seed won't grow, why should I waste my energy on it?"

If the gardener believes the seed can grow, he will expect it to do so. He will imagine the seed growing and bearing fruit, and so he will be compelled to take action to make sure that the seed matures. Now, imagine what would happen if the gardener believes and expects, but does not take action. Nature might withhold rain and the seed would dry out; intense heat could wither the leaves; floods could wash away the seed; insects may feast on the leaves; and so on and so forth. Without constant nurturing, that seed's fate is left to chance.

When what you creatively visualize reaches your subconscious mind, you will receive bursts of inspiration, spoken or visual messages, powerful urges, or hunches. It is vital that you take action on those instructions without delay. Most of the messages you receive from your subconscious are time-sensitive. That doesn't mean you have to drop everything you're doing and act on every hunch you get, but don't allow inertia to set in! Take that first step.

If you don't take action, you are essentially saying, "No, thanks" to your subconscious, and this gets stored there as a belief that a particular approach is not wanted. Inaction sends the message that you're not interested. Take a beginner's attitude and allow your inner guidance to show you the way.

Mapping out a plan to achieve your goals using your conscious mind will limit the possible outcomes. Remember, your conscious mind is restricted to the five senses and your past experiences and it will not have the infinite knowledge that the subconscious has. Therefore, let the subconscious mind do the planning. You should act according to your instincts.

For example, many people might limit the options of leading a healthier life by focusing on fad diets or magic pills, because they don't believe or are unaware of the unlimited possibilities that are available to live a healthy lifestyle using their subconscious mind.

The opportunities to act are always there, but many times, be it due to fear, doubts, or lack of self-confidence, many stop from taking the necessary action. See the law of attraction as a lifestyle and apply it continuously; not just when you need something. In that way, you will change every aspect of your life. Conquer your fears, take action, and involve yourself with situations which are in the same direction as your goal.

Many of us fail at manifesting because we don't realize we can control our thoughts and feelings. Your thoughts and feelings give you the power to energetically align yourself with what you want to bring into your life. It's not always easy. However, it is something you can develop with practice.

Good feelings come from good thoughts, while bad feelings come from bad thoughts. By controlling your feelings, you can make sure you always have the right thoughts. When you are feeling bad, you know your thoughts are going in the wrong direction — for example, many people struggle in manifesting success because they sabotage themselves. They approach opportunities with an air of desperation (from a place of lack), but that approach doesn't work because they are not aligned with what they desire. They want success, but their thoughts and feelings are saying, "I can't have success." That inner conflict spells disaster for their dreams.

You can turn this downward spiral into an upward spiral very quickly. Start thinking about the day you got your diploma, first paycheck, or some other event that brings a smile to your face. Make sure you bring up those good thoughts and then start thinking about all of the ways you can achieve what you want. Write them down! Even if none of those ideas are realistic (at the moment), or even possible (in your current way of thinking) know this — whatever your mind conceives and believes, it can achieve.

It's okay not to know it all! It's okay to say, "I have no idea how this will work," but as long as you believe, expect, imagine, and feel what you want, you will set the wheels of manifesting into motion!

How do thoughts, feelings, and beliefs affect the results of your reality?

Trust, good feelings, and happiness are the keys to allowing the law of attraction to work for you. You have to allow yourself to attract the right things by being happy. When you're happy, the world seems brighter, more cheerful, and helpful. When you're sad, it feels cold, gloomy, and lonely. Which attitude is going to attract what you want? Feel happy, feel positive about your ability to have what you desire, and trust that it will manifest.

An analogy to the law of attraction is how a magnet works. It attracts iron, but not paper or plastic. The law of attraction works the same way to attract resources, circumstances, and people in your life that can help you become successful; but the magnet works only if its atoms are aligned in one direction.

The higher the percentage of atoms aligned in one direction, the more powerful the magnet becomes. A weak magnet can attract only small pieces of iron but a powerful magnet can pull an entire building down.

In essence, attraction works like this: you have to be the one that attracts the circumstances, environment, opportunities, and people you need. Your beliefs have to be aligned with your desires. Your expectations have to match your desires. Your imagination has to create the most wonderfully compelling, exciting image of what you desire. In this way, you can effortlessly attract what you want.

I say effortlessly, because when you are doing what is right for you, when you love every second of every action that you take, it doesn't feel like work at all. It's no struggle, no effort. But it's not sitting around wishing and hoping! The key is action, fueled by happiness, enthusiasm, good energy, belief, and the expectation that what you desire is coming towards you at the speed of thought.

When your beliefs, expectations, mental images, and feelings are aligned in one direction, they create the pull necessary to attract the right resources. Remember, your doubts are like atoms in a weak magnet pointing in random directions. If you can replace them with the right beliefs, you can become a powerful magnet, pulling in everything needed to achieve success. This principle, in practice, can attract anything your heart desires.

The law of attraction has two parts – wanting something and having it. The first part, wanting, is easy, clear, and straightforward. It is your desire. It may be to own a new house or car, or to get a few thousand dollars, or to get a new career, or to win the partner of your dreams. The 'wanting' part of it just needs to be more vividly visualized.

The second part is that of having it. You begin by believing that you already have it, and you feel the happiness or gratitude of it being yours. This positive energy starts to work and attracts even more of that in your life. However, there is an energy that gives rise to that feeling, and if this energy is absent, the intention loses its power.

When you want something very badly, and you start to vibrate a lack of that and feel pessimistic about not having it, then you start to attract more of those negative circumstances.

These are the principles of the law of attraction. Remember that without taking action; there will be no results. Taking action is the key to manifesting your dreams.

The law of attraction is a surefire law. It works for everyone. If you are not able to attract what you desire, you need to allow your subconscious mind to give you the guidance needed.

 The good news is that by applying the law of attraction, you start to send positive thoughts and ideas to your subconscious mind and reprogram it. That will help you to believe in yourself and take action despite your possible fears. The law of attraction listens to your subconscious mind.

Think of your subconscious as a GPS. You enter your destination in it and it takes you there. There would be times when you wonder why it is asking you to turn left when you think (based on 'reality') that you should be turning right. But if you trust the GPS and let it do its job, it will guide you to your destination.

IN A NUTSHELL

- *Whether we are aware of it or not, the law of attraction is at work in our lives.*

- *Good feelings come from good thoughts, while bad feelings come from bad thoughts.*

- *Like attracts like. Good thoughts will attract good things and bad thoughts will attract bad things in our life.*

- *The only way to manifest something in your outer world is to improvise and amend your inner world, which includes your inner vibrations, thoughts, and emotions.*

- *You will effortlessly attract all the resources that you need to fulfill your desire if you choose to believe, expect, and imagine the right outcome.*

Chapter 14
ATTRACT AND MANIFEST

*"Whatever belief I am practicing, the Law of
Attraction will validate with evidence."*
— **Esther Hicks**

"I was craving pasta, and to my surprise, my wife made the same for dinner."

"I felt that I deserved a promotion, and surprisingly, amongst other deserving candidates, I got promoted."

"I was looking for a change in my job, and out of the blue it was offered to me."

Do you resonate with any of the above statements? You thought about something, and you got it! And when it happened, did you brush it off as a coincidence or a miracle?

Well, if you take a closer look at the sequence of events happening, it is nothing but the law of attraction at work. You wished for something and it manifested in your life. The process of attracting things and circumstances happens so harmoniously that you may spend your entire life without noticing it. Once you use your conscious mind to observe your thoughts and reality, you will understand how the process of attracting things works.

When we think of our strong desires with a conscious mind, then they are deeply submerged. People's desires are linked to their positive energy and it creates a belief in them. Over time, this belief becomes strong in them. By doing so, they attract these things to themselves.

The secret of manifestation lies in the feeling about the thing you wish to manifest in your life. Whenever you desire something and you feel good about it, you are feeding the thought with positive energies of love, joy, peace, abundance, and success. These vibrations begin to multiply, which then brings what you desire into your life. On the other hand, if you have feelings of guilt, worry, disappointment, resentment, fear, insecurity, doubt, hesitation, or sadness, you emit those vibrations which will attract negative situations into your life.

The law of attraction says that 'like attracts like.' So it means that positive thoughts will attract positive things in your life, while negative thoughts will attract negative things. Whatever you focus on grows. It is of vital importance to understand that your thoughts will shape your reality. Our mind is like a mirror. It will reflect whatever we think. The greatest secret of manifesting is realizing that every small thought, even those that may seem unimportant, contribute to shaping our life and manifesting our desires.

What you wish to attract in your life may come to you instantly and you might call it a miracle; or it may come indirectly, through various stages where one incident, event, or thought may lead to another, helping you eventually reach the end result. As I mentioned earlier, I desired to be rich and hence wanted to become a doctor. Well, that did not happen and while the sequence of events seemed random, they were beautifully woven together to ultimately help me reach my goal. Here are a few tips to attract and manifest your desires in your life based on my personal experiences.

- Once you desire something, make sure that your desire is strong and that you are motivated and committed enough to make it happen.

- Visualization plays an important role in the law of attraction. If you are not able to visualize the final product, develop the habit.

- You need to be persistent, disciplined, and focused. A restless mind cannot achieve anything.

- Once you desire something and send the message to the Universe, the process starts. The Universe will present opportunities in front of you from time to time. You need to be ready to take advantage of them.

- It is important to take action when you receive signals — such as a phone call, a job offer, a gut feeling, or advice from somebody — that strikes a chord within.

Having experienced the power of belief and attraction, I started using it consciously in my life. Our mentors, Kanti and Lata, had moved to Manalapan, New Jersey. When they bought their house and we visited them there, I said to Kanti, "I will buy a house next to yours so that we can be neighbors." But at that time the house next door was under construction and was already sold.

However, it just so happened that the person who had bought that house then backed out. The builder tried to sell it again but he did not succeed. Kanti called and asked me whether I would be interested in buying that house. How could I let go of this opportunity? The deal was done. But I needed to sell the house we were living in to be able to pay for that one. The real estate agent told me not to mention this to the builder as it might affect the deal. I told him not to worry, and that I would sell our existing house the very same day.

I had absolutely no clue how that was going to happen. I called the real estate agent in that area and the response was quite disappointing. She said that the chances of our house getting sold were very bleak, as no sales were happening in our area.

The same evening, Mina received a phone call from one of our old friends who had been out of touch for a long time. They spoke for a while and she hung up the phone. Mina later realized that this friend had mentioned awhile back that they were looking for a house in the area where we were currently living. She called her back and asked her if they were still looking to buy a house, because we were planning to sell ours. They were still in the market, and the deal was closed on the phone the same day. Everything fell into place and we bought our dream home.

This is how the power of belief, expectation, and imagination miraculously works. If you believe in something, you attract the right resources and people in your life that will help you achieve your goal.

IN A NUTSHELL

- *Ask, believe, and receive. Most importantly, it is your unshakable faith in what you ask for that will ultimately bring you what you ask.*

- *It is of vital importance to understand that your thoughts will shape your reality.*

- *The secret of manifestation lies in your feelings about the thing you wish to manifest in your life.*

- *Whatever you want to manifest, no matter how big or small it may be, it has to manifest when you believe in it, expect it to happen, and imagine having it now.*

- *There is no difference in the process to manifest big dreams compared to small dreams. Both are the same to the Universe. It's your thoughts that make it hard or easy.*

Chapter 15
TRUST AND ACKNOWLEDGE

"Watch your thoughts; they become words.
Watch your words; they become actions.
Watch your actions; they become habits.
Watch your habits; they become character.
Watch your character; for it becomes your destiny."
— *Upanishads*

Say that you are working for an organization and your boss assigns you some work. You know you are good at it and can successfully accomplish the given work. You begin the job, but intermittently, your boss comes and questions you, "Hey, would you be able to do it?" or "How long would you take to do it?"

When he asks you these questions, how would you feel? Probably irritated, right? You think, "Why can't he trust me?"

However, suppose your boss trusts you completely about the assignment he has given you. You would most likely happily and easily complete it in time. If your boss also acknowledges and is grateful for the work that you have done, you would feel like doing more good work the next time.

In the same way, when you ask the Universe for something that you know it is capable of creating, if you continually doubt its creative work you will be sabotaging its efforts. But if you instead trust that it will do its work for you and if you acknowledge those efforts in the process, what you want will easily come to you.

Trust and acknowledgment are key to allow the law of attraction to work for you.

The law of attraction is infallible. As soon as you ask for something, the Universe goes into action. It starts working on the process to get the desired thing to you. Then why does it not always happen? Perhaps we are blocking or resisting it from coming our way, consciously or unconsciously. And this happens mainly due to lack of trust.

It is important to trust that what you have asked for is yours and that the Universe will respond to your continual positive thoughts with positive results. You need to think, act, and speak in the present tense as though your request has been granted. When you combine this faith in the Universe with feelings of gratitude and visualization, you truly are multiplying the power of the law of attraction. Every positive step taken in faith and trust will lead to the manifestation of truly magnificent things.

The beliefs that you form also play an important role when it comes to trust. I always believed that whenever I needed money it would be provided. This belief was implanted in me by my mother, who would always say, "In your life, you may wake up hungry, but you will never go to bed hungry. Trust me on this."

This was an important belief that not only helped me build trust but also miraculously worked for me during every stage in my life. I would like to share an incident from my life that is a testimony to this. It happened when I was working at the Citibank. I had just gotten married and Mina and I were still working hard towards our goals. At that time, back in India, my elder brother had his own business. Unfortunately, the business didn't do so well and he suffered great losses.

In India, people generally think that if you have a relative working in America, they should be earning very well and can support you. One fine day I got a letter from by brother saying that he needed some amount of money. The amount my brother needed was greater than my annual income. I didn't have that kind of money at the time. However, I promised to help him, even though I didn't really know how. I had complete trust in the law of belief and law of attraction. I was confident that I would be provided with that money and I left the 'how' and 'when' to the Universe.

A few days later, my boss called me to his office and said, "Kulin, we are in the process of going through the accounts and the salary structure of our employees; and we noticed that you were promoted last year and we never raised your salary. So here is a check for your unpaid dues!"

I had never thought about a raise since I was happy with the work and the experience that I was getting. But my boss was afraid that I might leave the job and go elsewhere if my salary did not match my position. I was amazed at the timing at which this happened. The money I received was the exact amount I needed to send back home to my brother. I attracted the resources because of my belief. This is how the Universe works.

Many say they have complete trust, but the underlying feelings could be completely different. The best way to measure your trust is to examine your feelings. Feelings are a thought-measuring device. They tell us exactly what we are thinking and what frequency our thoughts are on in an instant. If you feel great and positive as though you have already received what you desired for, it means you have full trust in the process. The law of attraction is completely based on positive thoughts. Even a single negative thought will reduce its power. Hence the 'where,' 'when,' and 'how' of the manifestation should be totally left to the Universe to handle. You should feel very happy and comfortable with that which you aspire for.

The need to control, or that you must go through suffering to be rewarded, are negative beliefs so deeply ingrained in us since our childhood that they require some serious mental effort to overcome. We form many limiting beliefs based on our past experiences and our current reality. We will never be able attract what we want if we continue thinking these strong negative beliefs.

The key is to convert the limiting beliefs into empowering ones. The law of attraction is a process. As your awareness expands, your attitude shifts, empowering beliefs become more dominant, and your experiences will start to improve.

The second most important key to attract anything that you desire in your life is gratitude. How does it feel when someone appreciates and thanks you for everything you do for them? You feel great and positive, don't you? When writing official letters, when we have to request for a favor, we write 'thanking you in anticipation.' This means that we are expressing our gratitude towards the person even before our work is done. This also applies to the Universe. The law of attraction says that we should express gratitude for the thing we have asked for as if we have already received it.

If a person does have abundance but does not show gratitude, he will eventually lose it. This is because he is telling the Universe that he does not deserve it. When the Universe perceives this, it stops delivering.

On the other hand, if a person lacks abundance but shows gratitude for what he has, the Universe will in turn give more of what that person wishes. If a person both lacks abundance and does not show gratitude, he will continue to live in that way, because he has not shown that he deserves more.

Whenever you feel good about a certain thing in your life and you acknowledge it, a highly positive vibration is created which attracts more and more positive things in your life.

Remember that when you are consciously aware of your blessings and are grateful for them, you are focusing more clearly on what you do want and you are attracting more of those things into your life. Gratitude is more than just being thankful. It is a way of life. It is a conscious choice to focus on the blessings of life rather than to complain about shortcomings or problems.

Remember that whatever you focus on grows, expands, and multiplies in your life.

You may practice some affirmations of gratitude such as the following.

"I am grateful for all the comforts in my life."

"I am blessed to have such wonderful and loving people in my life."

"I am grateful for the home that I live in." "I am grateful that I am alive."

The list is endless. After all, we have so much to be grateful for. I have made a habit to list all the things that I am grateful before I go to sleep. This keeps me in a positive frame of mind no matter what has happened throughout the day.

If you desire wealth in your life, be grateful for what you have, even if you don't have enough. If you desire good relationships in your life, be aware of the loving and caring people around you. Thank them for being there for you and thank the Universe for surrounding you with such people. You will attract more of them.

Count your blessings and you will be blessed, and see how the law of attraction starts working magically for you.

IN A NUTSHELL

- *Trust and acknowledgment are key to allow the law of attraction to work for you.*

- *It is important to trust that what you have asked for is yours and that the Universe will respond to your continual positive thoughts with positive results.*

- *The law of attraction is always in operation, and it brings to each person the conditions and experiences that they think about, or those which they desire and expect.*

- *The law of attraction can help you experience a larger vision than you had ever imagined, and this is done through the power of your own thoughts and feelings.*

- *Most people will never achieve positive results using law of attraction because they do not trust and acknowledge the power of the Universe. They think positively, but deep down, their thoughts, words, and actions are not in sync with each other.*

IN CLOSING

Now that the four laws of success have been revealed, it's important to understand the power of happiness in order to activate those laws. Finding the right balance in every aspect of life is the key to a happy and content life. It is up to us to seek and find the right balance that works for us. An excess in one area of life and a lack in another will not help you achieve the happiness that you deserve. What good is your wealth if you don't have the right health to cherish it? What good is a long, healthy life without a soul mate or someone to cherish and share it with?

The right blend of health, wealth, relationships, and spiritual well-being can help you achieve everything that you set out to gain. You will be able to cherish your life in a better manner if you come across the right balance in life.

However, you can't expect to create drastic changes in each area all at once or overnight. Take it one step at a time, and if you feel overwhelmed by the process then it means you need to slow down. That's like running too many programs on your computer all at the same time — resulting in it crashing! A crash, in this case, means reverting to your old ways. Focus your attention on one thing at a time.

Let me emphasize it one more time: good habits are hard to develop but are easy to live with. Bad habits are easy to develop but are hard to live with.

In essence, you will create massive positive changes in your life by taking very small, incremental steps of building new thought patterns (or thought habits) that center around new, empowering beliefs, and expectations, and by consciously choosing happiness.

Start by choosing happiness. Then use the four laws of success to create life-changing beliefs. Stick with it. You are worth it! You matter!

Whatever success means to you, go for it. Whatever you set your sights on can be yours by following the steps outlined in this book. It's all about the journey, so make the journey one of fun, happiness, and great enthusiasm. Let your intuition guide you, take action on your intuitive guidance, allow the process to unfold, and reap the fruits of your desire.